Stopwatch

Student's Book & Workbook

5

Alastair Lane

Richmond

Richmond

58 St Aldates
Oxford
OX1 1ST
United Kingdom

Stopwatch Student's Book Level 5

First Edition: August 2016
ISBN: 978-607-06-1356-2

© Text: Alastair Lane
© Richmond Publishing, S.A. de C.V. 2016
Av. Río Mixcoac No. 274, Col. Acacias,
Del. Benito Juárez, C.P. 03240, Ciudad de México

Publisher: Justine Piekarowicz
Editorial Team: Griselda Cacho, Gabriela Pérez, Jacaranda Ruiz
Design Team: Jaime Ángeles, Karla Ávila, Daniel Mejía
Pre-Press Coordinator: Daniel Santillán
Pre-Press Team: Susana Alcántara, Virginia Arroyo
Cover Design: Karla Avila
Cover Photograph: © **Shutterstock** Ivan Smuk (Rowers in eight-oar rowing boats on the tranquil lake)

Illustrations: Alastair Lane pp.: 27, 32; Fabian de Jesus Ramírez pp.: 74, 75, 86, 94. Ismael Vásquez pp.: 8, 15, 16, 17, 25, 26, 31, 33, 37, 40, 42, 43, 48, 50, 54, 56, 58, 59, 65, 72, 87, 98, 99, 101, 102, 110, 114, 115, 120, 121, 141.

Photographs: © **AFP:** Jason Merrit GETTY IMAGES NORTH AMERICA AFP p.96 (Adele, center left), Philippe Giraud / Biosphoto, AFP p. 102 (Cooking Curanto, center right), LAFFORGUE Eric / hemis.fr / Hemis, AFP p. 102 (Festival of Easter Island In Tapati, center), Chris Jackson / Getty Images AsiaPac / Getty Images / AFP p. 105 (Hāngi A Traditional Māori Meal, right center), Mark Moffett / Minden Pictures / Biosphoto / AFP p. 104 (giant cricket, right center), Qin Cunguang / Imaginechina / AFP p. 113 (China Heilongjiang Kids Skating Training, center left), Kobal / The picture desk / AFP p. 113 (Stage direction, top center), Tristan Deschamps / Only France / AFP p. 113 (Graffity Artist, center), Jeffrey Rotman / Biosphoto / AFP p. 113 (Marine biologist, top right), Ben Torres / Getty Images North America / AFP p. 113 (Killed, top left), The Kobal Collection / Discovery Network / AFP p. 118 (Crab fishing, bottom right), The Kobal Collection / Discovery Network / AFP p. 118 (Crab fishing, bottom left), The Kobal Collection / Discovery Network / AFP p. 119 (Crab Fishing in Alaska, bottom), Kimihiro Hoshino / AFP p. 123 (Ryan Germick, center), Saul Loeb / AFP p. 124 (Cristeta, center right), Kevin Winter / Getty Images North America / AFP p. 124 (Andrew Stanton, center left), Michael Buckner / Getty Images North America / AFP p. 124 (Ishai Golan, bottom center), Jason Merritt / Getty Images North America / AFP p. 124 (Susan Wojcicki, bottom right).
© **Caters News Agency:** Caters News Agency / Chris Dyche p. 116 (LIU Bolin, "The Invisible Man 1", top left), Caters News Agency / Jamie Smith p. 116 (LIU Bolin, "The Invisible Man 2", bottom left), Caters News Agency / Jamie Smith p. 117 (LIU Bolin, "The Invisible Man 3", left).
© **Shutterstock.com:** Cloud Mine Amsterdam p. 14 (drummer, center bottom), Vira Mylyan-Monastyrska p. 14 (Festival Jazz Bez, center left), Andrea Raffin p. 14 (One Direction, center right), Hurricanehank p. 14 (Presentation of Scriptonite, center left), Silentwings p. 14 (festival at Konark, Orissa, India, Bottom right), Christian Bertrand p. 14 (Nile Rodgers at Sonar Festival, bottom right), Christian Bertrand p. 16 (drummer, center right), Jaguar PS p. 19 (Bruno Mars, center right), JStone p. 19 (Taylor Swift, bottom right), Yulia Grigoryeva p. 21 (heavy-metal band, bottom), Ryan Rodrick Beiler p. 22 (The Edge, guitarist of U2, center right), FlashStudio p. 22 (Westlife, center right), Jack.Q p. 23 (Riverdance, bottom left), Igor Bulgarin p. 28 (Members of the Theatre "Anthill", center right), Larry St. Pierre p. 28 (High school sailing team, center top), Vacclav p. 28 (a plane to Munich, center right), evantravels p.34 (Cappadocia, Turkey, bottom right), SJ Travel Photo and Video p. 35 (Hot air balloon fly, bottom), Aleph Studio p. 46 (tourists in mall, top left), Bplanet p. 49 (Chiang Mai Songkran festival, center right), topten22photo p. 49 (the splashing water with elephants, center right), Arina P Habich p. 70 (Denver Airport, top right), CP DC Press p. 70 (Aeroporto Santos Dumond, center), Komar p. 70 (passport control at airport, left), Rob Wilson p. 70 (an airline counter, top right), ChameleonsEye p. 70 (Passengers at Customs, center), Alexandra Lande p. 73 (Competitions taking part on the Klementieva, center right), Watcharee Suphaluxana p. 76 (Louvre Museum, center left), GongTo p.78 (TripAdvisor, center left), Komar p. 78 (Singapore International Airport, bottom left), withGod p. 80 (Safety operators at the Tan Son Nhat Airport, top right), Mirco Vacca p.82 (A Med toothpaste, center left), Settawat Udom p. 83 (People uses mobile phone, center right), Arseniy Krasnevsky p. 83 (Five little punks, top left), Neale Cousland p. 84 (Melbourne's graffiti, center), GTS Productions p. 84 (Street art, top left), Sanga Park p. 91 (Inside bus, center left), Sean Pavone p. 90 (The Myeong-Dong in Seoul, bottom left), tanuha2001 p. 93 (social media icons, right), Denis Makarenko p. 96 (Julia Roberts, bottom left), Helga Esteb p. 96 (Tom Hiddleston, bottom center), JStone p. 96 (James Corden, center), DanielW p. 97 (Times Square, top left), Ekaterina Pokrovsky p. 97 (Chinese New Year parade, top left), rehoboth foto p. 97 (river market, bottom left), Ventura p. 104 (Baldwin Street, New Zealand, center right), Paolo Bona p. 104 (the haka, maori traditional war dance, center right), Mark Moffett / Minden Pictures / Biosphoto p. 104 (giant cricket, right center), Migel p. 109 (San Fermin festival in Pamplona, center left), Andre Luiz Moreira p. 109 (The Carnival Samba competition, Rio de Janeiro, bottom left), Vitaly Ilyasov p.109 (The White Nights Festival, St. Petersburg, center left), Vintagepix p. 119 (A fisherman raises a steel crab trap in Alaska, center), ksl p. 122 (Lighting technician in Hamburg, center), Igor Bulgarin p. 131 (Members of the Dnepropetrovsk Youth Theatre "Verim", center), Yuri Turkov p.143 (The official playground of FC Barcelona, center left), R.M. Nunes p. 143 (Statue the Corcovado Mountain in Rio de Janeiro, center top), Paolo Bona p. 145 (The Western Walll separated Germany for 28 years, in Berlin, center right), tanuha2001 p. 151 (social media icons, center right), Stuart Monk p. 160 (Bus crossing Westminster Bridge in the United Kingdom, top left), Marcel Jancovic p. 167 (Girl against grafitti Wall, center left).

Images used under license from © **Shutterstock.com**
All rights reserved. No part of this work may be reproduced, stored in a retrieval system or transmitted in any form or by any means without prior written permission from the Publisher.

Richmond publications may contain links to third party websites or apps. We have no control over the content of these websites or apps, which may change frequently, and we are not responsible for the content or the way it may be used with our materials. Teachers and students are advised to exercise discretion when accessing the links.

The Publisher has made every effort to trace the owner of copyright material; however, the Publisher will correct any involuntary omission at the earliest opportunity.

Printed in Brazil by Forma Certa
Lote: 768446
Cod: 292713562

Contents

Student's Book

- **4** Scope and Sequence
- **7** Unit 0 Why do we learn English?
- **13** Unit 1 How does music affect you?
- **27** Unit 2 What have you done so far?
- **41** Unit 3 How do you help at home?
- **55** Unit 4 Are you lucky?
- **69** Unit 5 Where would you rather go?
- **83** Unit 6 Why do we behave the way we do?
- **97** Unit 7 What's it like in your country?
- **111** Unit 8 What's your dream job?

Workbook

- **126** Unit 1
- **130** Unit 2
- **134** Unit 3
- **138** Unit 4
- **142** Unit 5
- **146** Unit 6
- **150** Unit 7
- **154** Unit 8

- **158** Just for Fun Answer Key
- **159** Grammar Reference
- **168** Verb List

Scope and Sequence

Unit	Vocabulary	Grammar	Skills
0 Why do we learn English?	**Review:** aches and pains, habits, travel abroad	Present continuous; (future meaning) First conditional; Past simple and past continuous; Might, would; Should	**Listening:** Identifying specific information
1 How does music affect you?	**Music:** classical, country, jazz, Latin, pop, rap, reggae, rock, world music **Adjectives:** catchy, dramatic, inspiring, loud, moving, relaxing	Comparatives; Gerunds	**Listening:** Predicting meaning from pictures **Speaking:** Describing songs and feelings **Project:** Making a playlist
2 What have you done so far?	**Life Experiences:** camp overnight, change your look, design your own web page, learn to play a musical instrument, ride a horse, sail a boat, perform in a play, travel by plane	Present perfect; *For, how long, since*	**Writing:** Identifying signpost words in writing **Speaking:** Using signpost words in speaking **Project:** Making a board game with life experiences
3 How do you help at home?	**The Household:** cupboard, drawer, garbage, laundry, living room, tablecloth, trash, yard **Phrasal Verbs:** clean out, hang up, pick up, put away, take out, throw away, wash up, wipe off	Past perfect	**Listening:** Identifying specific information **Speaking:** Describing a household chores wheel **Project:** Performing a play about household chores
4 Are you lucky?	**Lucky Charms:** evil eye, fortune cat, fortune cookies, four-leaf clover, horse shoe, ladybug, rabbit's foot **Adverbs of Manner:** accidentally, badly, cleverly, deliberately, noisily, quickly, silently, slowly, stupidly, well	Second conditional	**Reading:** Identifying the author's audience and tone **Writing:** Writing to a specific audience and giving advice **Project:** Making a *Superstitions around the world* poster

Unit	Vocabulary	Grammar	Skills
5 **Where would you rather go?**	**Air Travel:** boarding pass, booking a flight, customs, luggage, passport, visa stamp **Human-made Wonders:** Angkor Wat, Colosseum, Blue Mosque, Machu Picchu, Great Wall of China, Moai statues, Ponte Vecchio, Pyramid of Giza	Preferences; Intensifiers; *Too, Enough*	**Listening:** Inferring relationships between events **Writing:** Using past forms to write a narrative **Project:** Making a traveler's guide
6 **Why do we behave the way we do?**	**Phrasal Verbs:** break up, figure out, get along, get over, give up, go on, keep it to yourself, turn in, own up, tell on someone	Could; May; Might	**Reading:** Reading moral dilemmas **Writing:** Using transition words for contradiction to write a solution to a moral dilemma **Project:** Debating about social media
7 **What's it like in your country?**	**Food Around the World:** Acarajé, Baklava, British lunch, Ceviche, Dim Sum, Goulash, Tandoori chicken **Cooking Verbs:** baking, boiling, frying, grilling, roasting, steaming **Adjectives:** bland, chewy, crispy, raw, sour, spicy, sticky	The passive; Present and past	**Listening:** Identifying supporting information **Writing:** Using correct capitalization and punctuation **Project:** Writing a recipe for a popular dish
8 **What's your dream job?**	**Unusual Jobs:** animation director, chef, sports coach, computer game programmer, crime scene investigator, graffiti artist, marine biologist, travel writer	Relative clauses; Defining, non-defining; *That, which, who*	**Reading:** Reading a magazine article **Writing:** Writing a summary **Project:** Organizing a tribe

Unit 0

1 Look at the pictures and complete the sentences with the words in the box.

(not) do anything   go to the beach   have a barbeque   play basketball   see the vet   take an exam

Sasha and Nick __are having a barbeque__ tonight.

Lamal _____ _____ tomorrow.

They _____ _____ this afternoon.

Tiger _____ _____ at 5 p.m.

We _____ _____ tomorrow.

I _____ _____ this evening.

2 Unscramble the illnesses to complete the conversations.

1. **A:** What's my temperature?
   B: It's 38 °C! You have a _____ (*refve*).

2. **A:** Ow! I hit my arm!
   B: Oh! You have a _____ (*suerib*). It's gone black!

3. **A:** I don't feel well. I have a _____ (*amcshtecoah*)
   B: I knew it was a bad idea to eat all that ice cream!

4. **A:** Do you have a cold?
   B: Yes, and I have a _____ (*nynur*) nose.

5. **A:** Can you turn that music off, please? I have a _____ (*aedehcha*).
   B: OK, and I'll get you an aspirin.

6. **A:** Why can't Rachel sing in the school concert?
   B: She has _____ (*orse*) throat. She can't even speak at the moment!

7. **A:** Your face is red!
   B: I know. I have a _____ (*nusbnur*).

8. **A:** Mom, I'm going to the store, OK?
   B: Oh, Mike, can you go to the drugstore for me? I need some _____ (*ecindemi*).

Stop and Think! How many reasons can you think of for learning English? Which is the most important to you?

3 Make the sentences true for you.

1. If I see a funny photo on the Internet, I'll _____.
2. If I don't have any homework tonight, I'll _____.
3. If it rains on Saturday, I won't _____.
4. If a new student joins our class next week, I'll _____.
5. I'll be happy tomorrow if _____.
6. My parents will be angry if _____.
7. I'll go out with my friends on Friday if _____.
8. I'll ask my parents for a new smartphone if _____.

4 Find 10 regular past simple verbs in the word search.

```
S T O P P E D Q Z B S X
X G B K L W U G U G T M
X W B U A H S L E W U W
V J G Q N V W T Z Z D C
Q O P E N E D R P H I L
Q K L Q E V H I J W E O
S K A X D K K E J R D S
T R Y R W J Q D H E X E
A Z E B H Z Z H X I K D
Y M D H W O R R I E D Z
E C J D R O P P E D Q B
D W C B X D S M I L E D
```

5 Complete the table with the verbs from Activity 4.

Spelling of Regular Past Simple Verbs			
+ed	+d	Double the final consonant e.g. p → pped	y → ied

6 Think Fast! Can you think of an irregular past simple verb that begins with these letters: A, B, C, D, F, G, H, K, M, P, S, T, W?

7 Circle the correct options to complete the sentences.

1. I didn't see the red light because I **looked / was looking** at my smartphone!
2. We had a sandwich for lunch and then we **had / were having** a donut for dessert.
3. We bought a new bag while we **shopped / were shopping** downtown.
4. When Ian **surfed / was surfing** the Internet, a virus shut down his computer.
5. I forgot to turn on my alarm clock, so I **didn't wake up / wasn't waking up** on time for school.
6. I took my umbrella to school because it **rained / was raining**.

8 🎧¹ Listen and complete the conversation.

Dom: I'm going to Peru with my parents.
Fran: Peru! Wow! (1) _____ you like to see the Nazca Lines?
Dom: The Nazca Lines? What are they?
Fran: They are giant drawings in the desert. You can't see them on the ground. You have to go up in a plane. Some experts think the Nazca Lines (2) _____ be 2,000 years old.
Dom: Are they just lines in the desert?
Fran: No, the Nazca Lines are drawings of animals and plants. Look at this photo. What does it look like?
Dom: Hmm… yes, it (3) _____ be an animal. I know! It's a monkey! So how many of these drawings are there?
Fran: About 70 designs, but they (4) _____ find more in the future. Archaeologists work there all the time.
Dom: Why did ancient people make these pictures?
Fran: There are lots of theories. One is that they (5) _____ help people communicate with aliens.
Dom: Aliens! No way! I (6) _____ like to see the Nazca Lines with my own eyes.
Fran: Well, their purpose is a mystery. (7) _____ your parents like to see them, too?
Dom: I think they (8) _____. We will go and I (9) _____ solve the mystery and become famous!
Fran: Good luck!

9 Complete the crossword puzzle.

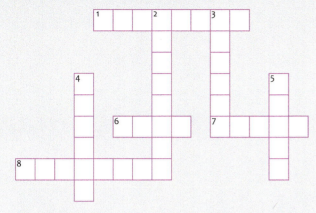

Across →

1. You need a _____ to travel to another country.
6. We're going on vacation and I'm going to _____ in a hotel for the first time!
7. I'm going to catch a _____ at the railway station.
8. I have dollars, but I need euros. Where can I _____ money?

Down ↓

2. When you go on vacation, you pack a _____ with your clothes.
3. When you go on vacation in the mountains, you can go to a ski _____.
4. We booked our _____ from New York to Rio online.
5. On vacation, we hired a tour _____ who took us around the city.

10 Circle the correct options to complete the blog.

B Improve Your Memory

forgetfulLulu

How can I improve my memory?
I'm thirteen and I have a lot of exams, but I can't remember anything! How can I improve my memory?
Please help me. What (1) **shouldn't / should** I do?
Lulu
Reply

Reply

First of all, Lulu, when you study, you (2) **should / shouldn't** just read things. When you learn some new information, you (3) **should / shouldn't** write it down. Many teens never write notes, but this is an essential aid to memory.
In addition, you (4) **should / shouldn't** try to remember everything at the same time. When a course has lots of facts, like history, you (5) **should / shouldn't** make some cards, and put one fact on each card. Then look at the cards from time to time to remember the information – you (6) **should / shouldn't** put them in your bag and forget about them!

The Experts

11 Complete the sentences with the words in the box.

| go hang keep order sleep stay stream work |

1. I want to be a writer one day, so I _____ a journal.
2. I don't watch TV, but I like to _____ movies on my tablet.
3. I don't like to _____ up late. I usually go to bed at 10 p.m.
4. We don't have a lot of money, but we _____ out to eat in a restaurant sometimes.
5. The best way to stay fit is to _____ out.
6. On Saturdays, I usually _____ out by inviting my friends to my house.
7. My parents hate cooking, so they like to _____ a take-out on the weekend.
8. I'm so tired on Sundays! I always _____ in and don't get up till 11!

Stop and Think! How does having a balance between school, hobbies, friends and family affect your learning process?

Vocabulary

1 🎧² **Listen and label the music categories for a new radio app.**

country
classical
Latin
jazz
world music
pop
rap
reggae
rock

Stop and Think! Is it easier to play classical or rock music?

2 Complete the sentences so they are true for you.

1. The music I like the most is _____.
2. The music I dislike the most is _____.
3. My parents' favorite music is _____.
4. I would like to learn to play _____ music.

3 Listen to a band talking about music. Circle the correct answer.

1. The band's name is **Green** / **Orange** Dream.
2. The concert is next **weekend** / **month**.
3. They have to choose **one song** / **two songs** for the school concert.
4. They talk about the song **"Can You Feel The Love Tonight?"** / **"Circle of Life"** from *The Lion King*.
5. In the end, they choose a **reggae** / **rap** song.

4 Complete the sentences with these words to describe music. Then listen again to check.

inspiring   loud   moving   relaxing   catchy   dramatic

1. It's a country song. It's a _____ tune. People cry when they hear it.
2. We need some _____ songs. Music that people can remember and sing along to.
3. She likes to listen to _____ music when she has breakfast.
4. I love the music from *The Lion King*. It's so _____, so exciting!
5. We're a rock band. We play _____ music. Guitars! Drums! Noise!
6. I want to do a song that's _____. You know, a song that gives you hope and ideas.

5 Think Fast! In your notebook, write an example of a song you play loud, a song that's moving, a catchy song and a relaxing song. Then write down the music category for each song.

Guess What! Reggae comes from the island of Jamaica in the Caribbean. Its most famous singer was Bob Marley (1945–1981).

15

Grammar

1. 🎧⁴ **Look at the announcement. Then listen to the audition and complete the table.**

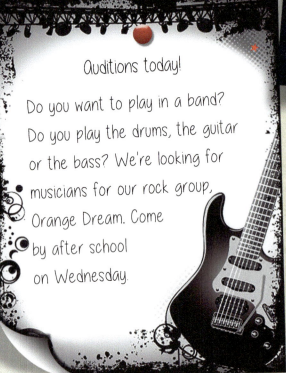

Auditions today!

Do you want to play in a band? Do you play the drums, the guitar or the bass? We're looking for musicians for our rock group, Orange Dream. Come by after school on Wednesday.

Name	Instrument	Does he / she pass the audition?
Emily		
Nick		
Dan		
Alex		

2. **Complete the sentences with the correct adjectives. Listen again to check.**

   difficult   good   old

   1. I'm as _____ as you. I'm 15 too!
   2. My brother isn't as _____ as me on the guitar.
   3. The bass isn't as _____ as the guitar.

as ... as

Emily's drums are **as big as** her.

3. **Circle your opinion. Explain your choices.**
   1. Playing the guitar is **as easy as** / **not as easy** as playing the piano.
   2. Dancing is **as fun as** / **not as fun** as playing football.
   3. Reading in English is **as difficult as** / **not as difficult as** listening in English.
   4. Smartphones are **as good as** / **not as good as** tablets.
   5. Having toast for breakfast is **as healthy as** / **not as healthy as** having cereal.
   6. Being late for school is **as bad as** / **not as bad as** not doing your homework.

not as ... as

Emily's not as tall as Chris.

4 Look and complete Zoe's reply.

1. Well, I want to play in the orchestra. The orchestra's (≠, popular) _____ our band, but I want to be a classical musician.
2. I know classical music's (≠, cool) _____ rock, but I can play solo in the orchestra.
3. Playing in the band's (≠, fun) _____ playing solo.
4. I know you will find someone who's (=, good) _____ me to take my place!

5 Complete the sentences with a noun or a gerund.

Nouns		
The orchestra	The band	Jazz

Gerunds	
Playing	Listening

1. _____ isn't as cool as the band.
2. _____ the drums is as difficult as playing the guitar.
3. _____ is as relaxing as classical music.
4. _____ isn't as fun as the orchestra.
5. _____ to pop music is as fun as listening to rock music.

6 Complete these sentences with your ideas.

1. _____ isn't as strong as _____.
2. _____ is as important as _____.
3. _____ is as famous as _____.
4. _____ isn't as delicious as _____.
5. I'm as _____ as _____.

Listening & Speaking

1 🎧⁵ **Look at the pictures and the title of a podcast. Write what you think it will be about.**

Be Strategic!
Before you listen, look carefully at any pictures that accompany the recording, e.g., on a web page for a podcast. These can help you predict the meaning.

I think the podcast will be about …

_____
_____
_____

2 Listen and check your answer.

3 Circle five mistakes in this summary of the conversation. Then listen again to check.

Megan and Josh discuss five ways that music affects our brains. First of all, music helps us to study. This is because when we listen to music we have to concentrate less. However, loud music is very **distracting**. Music also helps when we do sports. If we listen to music when we exercise, we don't notice messages from the brain that tell us to relax. Jazz is the best music for sports.

Music helps us learn languages. Megan listens to a lot of reggae and it helps her to learn Spanish. It's clear that music is essential in education; in fact, Megan thinks it is as important as English.

4 🎧⁶ **Guess the missing words in the comments. Then listen and check.**

When I _____, I listen to classical music. There aren't any words, so I don't find it distracting.

Before I take an English _____, I listen to English songs to help me prepare. I like One Direction best.

When I go to the _____, I listen to Taylor Swift on my headphones. I love her music when I'm running. I play it loud!

When I get ready to go out in the _____, I always put on catchy songs like "Uptown Funk" by Bruno Mars.

My parents go to a _____ class where they listen to country music and wear cowboy hats. It's so embarrassing!

My _____ play all this world music from Africa and Asia. They live next door, so I hear it all the time!

5 **Work in pairs. Think of songs to go with your feelings. Use these notes to help you.**

① A catchy song that you remember and sing along to.
_____
_____

② An inspiring song to listen to before you do something difficult.
_____
_____

③ A moving song for when you are feeling sad.
_____
_____

④ A dramatic song to listen to that is exciting.
_____
_____

⑤ A relaxing song to listen to when you study.
_____
_____

⑥ A loud song to play at a party.
_____
_____

Glossary

distracting: something which stops you from thinking or concentrating on a job

1 **Think Fast!** In your notebook, make a list of capital cities around the world. How many of your capital cities are in Europe?

2 Read the article. Find the information below.

THE BERLIN FESTIVAL

Founded in 2005, the Berlin Festival draws music fans from all over the world to listen to the best in electronic pop. The site of the festival is the old Berlin airport. It is a big open space where people can party all night long. Germany has always been the center of techno. The pioneers of this music form, Kraftwerk, were a German group from the 1970s. They were one of the first groups to record songs with no traditional instruments, only electronic ones. Today, German groups continue to rock the **crowds** with these futuristic sounds. The festival is a welcoming place for kids as well as adults. There are magicians, street artists and acrobats to see when there are no groups on the stage. The only problem for visitors is that there are no **camping facilities** at the festival. Visitors have to stay in hotels, which means that it can be expensive to visit.

1. The year that the Berlin Festival started _____
2. The type of music that they play at the festival _____
3. The location of the Berlin Festival _____
4. A famous band from Germany _____
5. Other attractions at the festival _____
6. The type of accommodation at the festival _____

Glossary

crowd: a large group of people who are together in a place

camping facilities: a place specially designed for setting up tents

3 Match the highlighted words in the text to the definitions.

1. _____: the location where an event happens
2. _____: the place where performers stand at a concert or in the theater
3. _____: attract people to go to a place or event
4. _____: the first people to do something

4 Look again at the Berlin Festival. Mark (✓) the parts of the festival each group of people might like. Compare and discuss your answers with a partner.

	Classical musicians	Families	People who live in your country	Rap fans	People in their 40s	Me!
Electronic pop						
Staying up late						
Big crowds						
Magicians and acrobats						

Guess What!
From 1949–1990, there were two countries called Germany. The country was divided after the Second World War. East Germany was communist. West Germany was a democracy.

Project

1 Match the descriptions to the photos.

1. ☐ One of the biggest rock bands in the world, U2, come from Ireland. Their lead singer is Bono and their most famous album is *The Joshua Tree* from 1987.
2. ☐ Galway is a particularly famous place to see live Irish music. It is an area in the west of Ireland next to the sea.
3. ☐ Ireland is famous all over the world for its music. Traditional Irish music often features a fiddle, a type of violin which people play very fast.
4. ☐ Ireland is also famous for dance, especially the musical *Riverdance*. Dancers stand in a line on stage and dance while staying in the same place and moving their legs in the air.
5. ☐ Ireland is not just famous for traditional music. Lots of pop groups also come from there, like *Westlife*. It's one of the world's most famous boy bands.

a

b

c

2 Read the sentences again and answer the questions.

1. What kind of band is U2?
   _____.

2. Where is Galway?
   _____.

3. What instrument is used in traditional Irish music?
   _____.

4. What Irish show can you see in a theater?
   _____.

5. What modern music comes from Ireland?
   _____.

Music from my country

3 Work in small groups. Create a project on music from your country. First, write an introduction to music from your country like the sentences in Activity 1. Think of:
- famous singers
- famous groups
- typical instruments
- famous songs
- a popular or traditional dance
- a place that is famous for music

4 Now prepare a playlist to tell people about the music from your country. Use your ideas in 3 to help you. Think about classical, traditional, rock, pop and dance. Choose about five songs.

5 Now present your playlist to the class. Explain why you chose the pieces of music. Did everyone in the class choose the same music? Why / Why not?

Our playlist introduces the music of …

_____.

The first item on our playlist is …

_____.

We chose this piece of music because …

_____.

In conclusion, our country's music is famous / popular / wonderful because …

_____.

 **Stop and Think!** What are some other places that are famous for their music?

Review

1 Order the letters to make music words.

1. A: I hate _____ (*norytuc*) music! It's so uncool.
   B: I don't like the music, but I like the fashion. I love wearing cowboy hats!
2. A: Do you know any famous films about _____ (*nalti*) music?
   B: Yes, there's an old one called *Buena Vista Social Club* about musicians in Cuba.
3. A: Do you ever listen to _____ (*drowl*) music?
   B: Yes, I do. I really like African music from Mali.
4. A: What is _____ (*gargee*)?
   B: It's a type of music from the Caribbean, especially Jamaica.
5. A: Wow! You have a saxophone!
   B: Yes. I play in a _____ (*zajz*) band now.
6. A: What music should we play at the party?
   B: _____ (*ppo*) music, because everyone likes that.
7. A: We need a guitar player for our _____ (*cork*) band. Can you play?
   B: No, but my sister can. She's an amazing guitarist!

2 Match to make sentences.

1. ☐ Latin   3. ☐ Classical music   5. ☐ Jazz
2. ☐ Rap   4. ☐ Pop music   6. ☐ Country

a. is often very old, for example, opera.
b. singers usually speak more than sing, and they speak very fast in the song.
c. music is from the US. People often sing sad songs about relationships.
d. most common instruments are saxophone, trumpet, piano, drums and guitar.
e. isn't one type of music. It describes lots of different music from countries in North, Central and South America.
f. enjoyable and catchy.

3 Read the sentences and circle the correct emoticon.

1. Why is that music so loud? I'm trying to get to sleep!
2. This song is really inspiring. We always listen to it before a big game.
3. I play this music before I go to bed. It's very relaxing.
4. This song is really catchy. I listened to it this morning, but now I can't get it out of my head!
5. The musical was amazing. The last song was really dramatic. I couldn't sit in my chair!
6. She sang a very moving song and everyone started crying.

4 Unscramble the sentences.

1. as / brother / as / tall / I'm / older / my
   _____

2. you / intelligent / isn't / as / Jack / as
   _____

3. Paris and New York / rainy / as / as / London / are
   _____

4. isn't / as / us / old / as / Payton
   _____

5. as / football / is / sports / good / as / other
   _____

6. long / as / a / is / meter / as / centimeters / 100
   _____

5 Complete the interview with the adjectives below. Then listen and check.

good   long   loud   round   scared   tall   white

A: So, you say you saw an alien?
B: Yes, I did.
A: What happened?
B: First, I saw the spaceship. It was as (1) _____ as a ball. It landed and this door opened. There was a terrible noise–it was as (2) _____ as an electric guitar.
A: What did the alien look like?
B: It was as (3) _____ as me, about two meters. Its neck was a (4) _____ as a giraffe's!

A: What color was it?
B: It was as (5) _____ as snow.
A: Did it speak English?
B: Yes, its English was as (6) _____ as yours or mine.
A: What did it say?
B: "Take me to your leader!"
A: How did you feel?
B: Terrified! Everyone was as (7) _____ as me!

6 Complete these common *as ... as* expressions with the words below.

cold   dry   easy   light   quick   red

1. The math homework was as _____ as "ABC." I did it in five minutes!
2. I love your car. It's as _____ as blood.
3. Your hands are as _____ as ice! Come inside and get warm!
4. It last rained six weeks ago. The garden is as _____ as a bone.
5. I opened the door and as _____ as a flash, the dog ran out. I couldn't stop her.
6. The bag isn't heavy. It's as _____ as a feather.

Just for Fun

1 Circle eight more types of music in the word snake.

(worldmusic)jazzclassicalrapreggaecountryrocklatinpop

2 Complete the puzzle. Which is the musical instrument in the purple grids?

1. You feel strong emotions when you listen to _____ music.
2. The opposite of *quiet*. _____
3. You listen to _____ music when you need to feel calm.
4. They use _____ music at exciting moments in movies.
5. A _____ song is one that people start singing when they hear it.
6. _____ music makes people believe they can do special things.

26

3 Write *as … as* sentences for the superhero. Use the words in the box.

brave   clever   fast   strong   quiet   tall

Vocabulary

1 Label the pictures with the words in the box.

camp overnight   change your look
design your own web page
learn to play a musical instrument
perform in a play   ride a horse   sail a boat
travel by plane

1 _____ 2 _____ 3 _____ 4 _____

5 _____ 6 _____ 7 _____ 8 _____

2 Complete the survey.

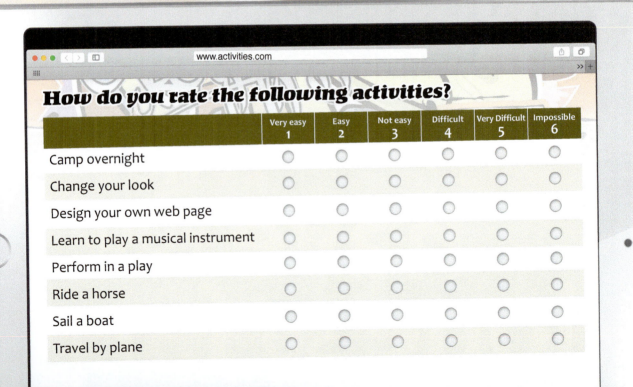

3 🎧⁷ Listen. What activities in Activity 1 are the people doing?

1. _____
2. _____
3. _____
4. _____
5. _____
6. _____
7. _____
8. _____

Guess What!
18% of US adults have never flown in a plane.

4 Look at the pictures in Activity 1. In pairs, discuss which ones you have done.

5 Discuss these questions.
1. Do you prefer camping overnight or staying at home? Why?
2. Do you know someone who changed their look? What did he / she do?
3. Do you know someone who has their own web page? What is on it?
4. What is the first musical instrument that people learn to play? Can you play it?
5. Do people perform in plays at your school? When? If not, why not?
6. You can ride a horse, but what other things can you ride?
7. Is it possible to sail a boat near where you live? Where?
8. Do you know anyone who is scared of flying in a plane? How does he / she usually travel?

Glossary
dye: to artificially change the color of something, e.g., your hair
give up: to stop doing something because it is too difficult

Grammar

1 Read the text. Discuss what you learn about the categories below.

1. Josh's family
2. his hobbies
3. his hopes for the future
4. his hometown
5. his achievements

6 FACTS ABOUT ME

I'm Josh Baker. I'm 13 and I'm from Cincinnati, Ohio. Here are 6 facts about me.

1 I have a **twin** sister, Joanne! And no, we're not identical.

2 I've been a fan of the Cincinnati Bengals my whole life. They've never won the Super Bowl. ☹ I've written a blog about the Bengals for two years.

3 Cincinnati is miles from the sea, so I've never swum in the ocean. That's my dream.

4 I speak Dutch. Really! My grandma comes from Holland and she's taught me some words. She's lived in the US since 1999.

5 I've been on TV! I ride a horse in a riding club and we won a competition. We appeared on the local news last month.

6 I've seen a bear! I went camping with my cousin last year and we saw a grizzly. It… was… enormous!

2 Look at the sentences and answer the questions.

1. Which ones are in the Past Simple?
2. Do we know when each action happened?
3. Which ones are about Josh's whole life up to now?
4. Which sentences use the Present Perfect and not the Past Simple?

a. *I've never swum in the ocean.*
b. *I've been on TV!*
c. *We appeared on the local news last month.*
d. *I went camping with my cousin last year.*

3 Look again at Activity 1. Write the past participles of these verbs. Are they regular or irregular?

be _____   swim _____
write _____   teach _____
see _____   win _____

Glossary
twin: two children born at the same time to the same mother

4 🎧⁸ **Listen to Josh and his friend Ashley talking about his favorite sports team. Complete the missing words.**

1. ASHLEY: How long _____ you _____ a fan of the Cincinnati Bengals?

   JOSH: I've been a Bengals fan for years. All my life!

2. ASHLEY: _____ you ever _____ them play in the stadium?

   JOSH: Yes, I _____. Three times!

3. ASHLEY: _____ you ever _____ any of the players?

   JOSH: No, I _____, but I hope I will one day.

4. ASHLEY: _____ the Bengals ever _____ the Super Bowl?

   JOSH: No, they _____! But they have been close.

Present Perfect

Have / has + past participle
I've been a fan of the Cincinnati Bengals my whole life.
They've never won the Super Bowl.
Have the Bengals ever won the Super Bowl?
How long have you been a fan?

Guess What!
We use *for* to say *how long* we have done something.
We use *since* to say *when* we did something.

5 **Complete the sentences with *for* or *since*.**

1. The Cincinnati Bengals have been a team _____ 1968.
2. Marvin Lewis has been the team's longest head coach _____ 13 seasons.
3. The team has played at the Paul Brown Stadium _____ 2000.
4. They haven't been close to winning a Super Bowl _____ 1989.
5. They reached the playoffs _____ four years from 2011–2014.

6 **Use the prompts to ask questions to a partner.**

1. How long / family / live / current home
2. How long / be / student / at this school
3. How long / know / your best friend
4. How long / sit / at same desk / classroom
5. How long / English teacher / teach your class

7 **Write three facts about you, your family or your life. Then share them with your partner and ask *how long* questions.**

Reading & Writing

1 Discuss these questions.

1. Have you ever drawn a picture of a friend or a famous person? Was it easy or difficult?
2. Do you think anyone can draw?
3. Do you have a favorite artist? Why do you like him / her?

2 Look at the sketches. Number the steps from 1–7.

a. Thirdly, draw the mouth and neck. _____
b. Next, you draw the hair. Don't forget to connect the hair to the eyes with the forehead. _____
c. First of all, you draw a circle in the center of the picture. This is the eye. _____
d. Finally, draw a speech bubble around the words and connect it to your person. Your cartoon is now finished. _____
e. After that, draw the ear. It's a good idea to put it at the same level as the eyes. _____
f. Then you write some words for your person to say. Always write the letters first so you know how much space you need. _____
g. Secondly, you put a dot in the eye and you draw the nose. _____

3 Circle seven signpost words or phrases in Activity 2.

4 Cover the text. Look at the sketches only. Can you remember all the instructions? Read the text again to check.

5 Work in pairs. Follow the steps to draw a cartoon of your partner. Is it easy or difficult?

6 In your notebook, use the pictures to explain how to set up a tent. Write the steps. Use signpost words.

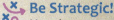
Be Strategic!
Use signpost words in speaking and writing to explain a process. These are words like *first of all, secondly, ...*

Choose a good location for your tent.

Clean the ground of sticks and stones.

Put a **tarp** on the ground.

Unroll the tent.

Assemble the tent poles.

Insert the poles into the material of the tent.

Put the poles in the ground to raise the tent.

Put **pegs** in the ground for the four corners of your tent.

Connect the tent poles to the pegs.
Your tent is now ready!

Glossary
tarp: a large piece of plastic or cloth that water cannot go through
pegs: a stick made of metal or wood that has a sharp end

Culture

3 min

1 Think Fast! How many different methods of transportation can you think of? Have you traveled in any / all of these?

2 Read about Cappadocia in Turkey. Underline three activities that people can do there.

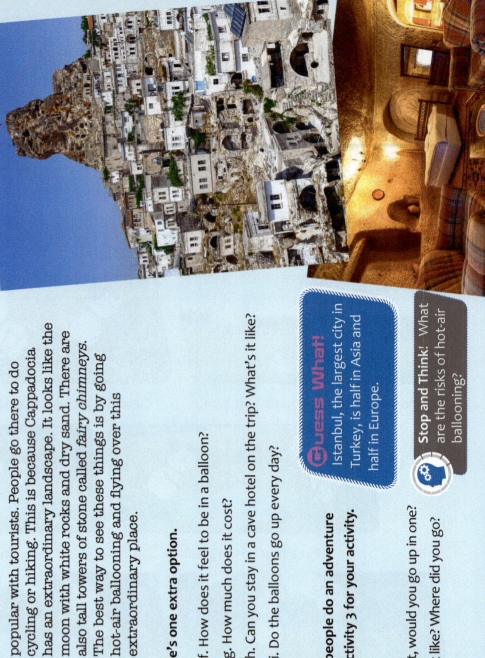

Turkey — Cappadocia

Cappadocia

Cappadocia is a region of Turkey in Central Asia. It's a very old place. People have lived there for thousands of years. In the past, people lived in homes in the rocks that were similar to **caves**. Nowadays, local people have converted their ancient homes into hotels for tourists. Cappadocia is very remote. It is several hours away from the nearest town, but it is still very popular with tourists. People go there to do cycling or hiking. This is because Cappadocia has an extraordinary landscape. It looks like the moon with white rocks and dry sand. There are also tall towers of stone called *fairy chimneys*. The best way to see these things is by going hot-air ballooning and flying over this extraordinary place.

3 Complete the article on page 35 with questions a–i. There's one extra option.

a. Is it safe to fly?
b. How long is the trip in the balloon?
c. How many times have you been in a hot-air balloon?
d. How do you get there?
e. Would you recommend it?
f. How does it feel to be in a balloon?
g. How much does it cost?
h. Can you stay in a cave hotel on the trip? What's it like?
i. Do the balloons go up every day?

4 Think about a place in your country or local area where people do an adventure activity like hot-air ballooning. Answer the questions in Activity 3 for your activity.

5 Discuss these questions.
1. Have you ever gone up in a hot-air balloon? If you haven't, would you go up in one?
2. Have you ever done a very long bus journey? What was it like? Where did you go?
3. Have you ever had a once-in-a-lifetime experience?

Guess What! Istanbul, the largest city in Turkey, is half in Asia and half in Europe.

Stop and Think: What are the risks of hot-air ballooning?

34

Hot-air Ballooning in Cappadocia

Q: (1) _____

A: Most people arrive in Turkey in Istanbul. Then you can get a flight to a town in Cappadocia. Alternatively, you can take a bus from Istanbul—the journey takes about 10 to 12 hours!

Q: (2) _____

A: Yes, and it's lots of fun. However, this is not modern accommodation. The **ceiling** is very low, so the accommodation isn't very comfortable for tall people! The walls are also made of rock, so it really feels like living underground.

Q: (3) _____

A: It's expensive. It's over $125 per person. It's worth it because it's a once-in-a-lifetime experience.

Q: (4) _____

A: Yes, it is. The pilots are all professionals with the right qualifications. People have gone up in hot-air balloons for over 200 years!

Q: (5) _____

A: It's about an hour, but it begins very early in the morning, often at 5 or 6 a.m.

Q: (6) _____

A: It's quite frightening at first because the basket is not very large and you are standing on a very thin floor. However, the views of the canyons and mountains are **breathtaking**, so you soon forget that you are flying in the air and you just enjoy the ride.

Q: (7) _____

A: No, they don't. The balloons cannot go up in bad weather, such as rain or strong wind. However, they do balloon rides all year round, but if you go in winter, you need a very warm coat and a scarf. You're in the mountains here!

Q: (8) _____

A: Absolutely! It's the best thing I've ever done!

Glossary

cave: a natural hole in rock that people or animals can use as a home

ceiling: the top part of a room

breathtaking: beautiful and amazing (e.g. a view or an experience)

Project

1 🎧⁹ Listen and mark (✓) the activities Bailey has done.

2 **Work in pairs. Check your answers in Activity 1.**

A: *Has Bailey helped someone stung by jellyfish?*
B: *Yes, she has. / No, she hasn't.*

3 **In groups, think of three things that you have done in your life that the other students have never done. Write** *have you ever* **questions for each one.**

I've been to Paris – Have you ever been to Paris?

I've gone to Canada on a student exchange program – Have you ever gone on a student exchange program?

4 **Complete the board game with the questions in Activity 3. Add more** *have you ever* **questions.**

5 **Use the board game as a draft and follow the steps.**

Step 1: Copy the board game on a bigger piece of cardboard paper.

Step 2: Add your own pictures or drawings to illustrate each question.

Step 3: Exchange board games with another group.

6 **Play the game in pairs. Find a counter to represent you. Toss a coin to move. Heads = 1 square. Tails = 2 squares. Discuss the question in the square.**

A: *Have you ever gone up in a hot-air balloon?*
B: *Yes, I have.*
A: *When did you go up in a hot-air balloon?*
B: *It was last year. I was on vacation with my parents…*

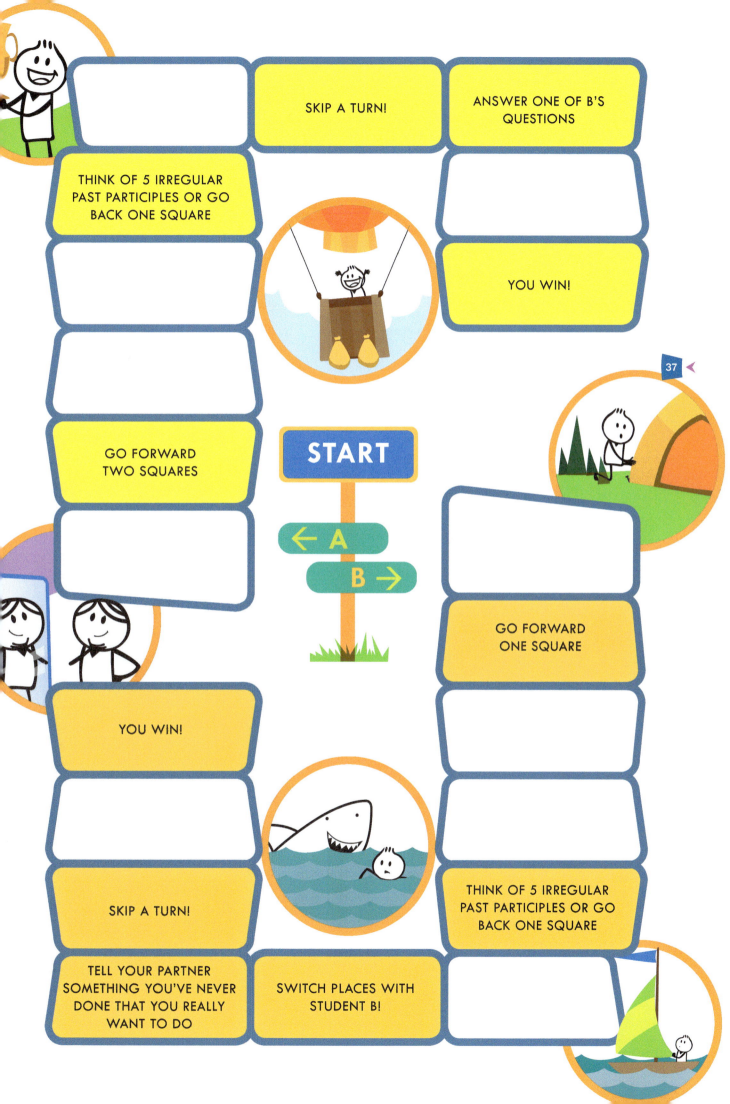

Review

1 Find six activities in the word snake. Then match them to the correct pictures.

rideahorseplaythedrumschangemylooktravelbyplanesailaboatcampovernight

1
2
3
4
5
6

▶ 38

2 Replace the words in bold with these words.

| her bike   a magazine   an opera   for a week   her hair   in a helicopter   the bass   paddle the canoe |

1. We camped in a tent **overnight** and it was cold!
2. My grandma is a singer. She's performing in **a play** in the city center.
3. Can you help me design **a web page**?
4. How often does she ride **her horse**?
5. I'm learning to play **the piano**, but it isn't easy.
6. It's was only when we were at sea that I admitted that I didn't know how to **sail the boat**!
7. She changes **her look** every week.
8. We traveled **by plane** over the city.

3 🎧¹⁰ Listen to five conversations. Write the number of each conversation.

a. sailing a boat   _____
b. camping overnight   _____
c. changing his / her look _____
d. traveling by plane   _____
e. performing in a play   _____

4 Underline the correct option to complete the conversation.

A: (1) **Have you ever driven / Did you ever drive** a go-kart?
B: Yes. I do it every weekend!
A: (2) **Have you won / Did you win** any races?
B: Yes, (3) **I've won / I won** five races. (4) **I've won / I won** one last weekend!
A: (5) **Have you had / Did you have** any accidents?
B: Yes, (6) **I've had / I had** an accident last year. (7) **I've crashed / I crashed** my kart!
A: (8) **Did you go / Have you gone** to the hospital after the accident?
B: No, (9) **I've never been / I never was** in the hospital in my life.
A: Lucky you! (10) **I broke / I've broken** my leg once and (11) **I spent / I've spent** three months in the hospital!
B: (12) **I've never broken / I never broke** a leg or an arm or anything. I guess I'm just lucky.

5 Complete the sentences using the Present Perfect.

1. I _____ (never / be) to Europe. I'd love to go there one day.
2. My mom _____ (meet) the president of the US! We have a photo of them in our living room.
3. My family _____ (move) four times in my life.
4. It _____ (not / rain) in our city this year! Everyone is worried about it.
5. We _____ (learn) a lot of new English words in our course so far.
6. My dog _____ (disappear)! We don't know where he is!
7. Dad _____ (lose) his smartphone. Can you help us look for it?
8. Mom _____ (not / come) home. I think she's still at work.

6 Complete the e-mail with *for* or *since*.

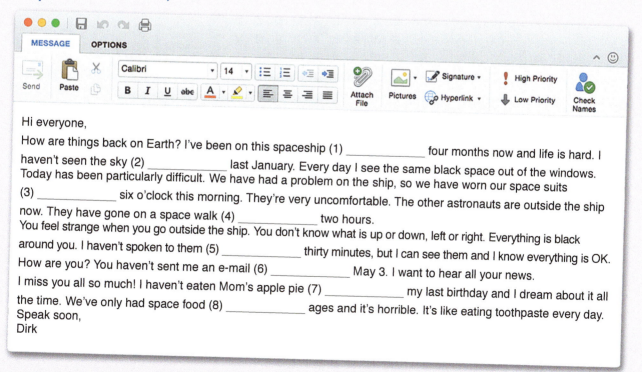

Hi everyone,
How are things back on Earth? I've been on this spaceship (1) _____ four months now and life is hard. I haven't seen the sky (2) _____ last January. Every day I see the same black space out of the windows. Today has been particularly difficult. We have had a problem on the ship, so we have worn our space suits (3) _____ six o'clock this morning. They're very uncomfortable. The other astronauts are outside the ship now. They have gone on a space walk (4) _____ two hours. You feel strange when you go outside the ship. You don't know what is up or down, left or right. Everything is black around you. I haven't spoken to them (5) _____ thirty minutes, but I can see them and I know everything is OK. How are you? You haven't sent me an e-mail (6) _____ May 3. I want to hear all your news. I miss you all so much! I haven't eaten Mom's apple pie (7) _____ my last birthday and I dream about it all the time. We've only had space food (8) _____ ages and it's horrible. It's like eating toothpaste every day.
Speak soon,
Dirk

1 **Cross out the wrong word in each sentence.**

1. I'm going to camp **in a tent / overnight / in the mall** tomorrow.
2. I usually ride my **bike / pig / horse** on the weekend.
3. I have wanted to learn to play the **drums / guitar / nose** for years!
4. I've never performed **in a math class / in a play / in the theater** before.
5. We sailed in a **boat / ferry / fish** for the first time on vacation!
6. It costs a lot of money to travel by **bird / plane / train**.
7. I want to change my **face / hair / look**. Do you have any ideas?
8. I've been in this **class / month / school** since the year began.

2 **Find 10 irregular past participles. Words can be horizontal or vertical.**

```
B E E N Q J T X W Z
X W H Z W K H P U T
D V A R K H O J Q B
R J D B R O U G H T
U D Q T Y X G V V B
N R R A I D H S U R
K I X W W K T E X O
J V M Q Z J M E R K
K E Z R E A D Q Z E
Z N W R I T T E N N
```

3 **Complete the questions with the correct form of the verb. Then add two questions to the list.**

Have you ever...	Student's name
1. _____ (eat) an insect?	_____
2. _____ (break) your arm?	_____
3. _____ (meet) someone from the US?	_____
4. _____ (find) some money in the street?	_____
5. _____ (travel) in a helicopter?	_____
6. _____ (see) a jaguar?	_____
7. _____	_____
8. _____	_____

4 Go around the class. Find one student who answers *yes* to each question. Write his or her name in the list.

Vocabulary

1. Listen and circle the correct option.

Household Chores

1. take out / off

2. pick away / up

3. hang on / up

4. throw away / off

Phrasal Verbs

A phrasal verb is a verb + particle (a word like *on*, *up* or *over*). The particle changes the meaning of the verb for example: *give up*.

This activity is too difficult! I give up!

2. Look at Activity 1 and write the phrasal verbs next to their definitions.

1. _____ : to get rid of something that you no longer want
2. _____ : to make a place clean by removing objects that are not wanted
3. _____ : to put something in the place where you usually keep it when you are not using it
4. _____ : to clean (someone or something) by using a towel, one's hand, etc.
5. _____ : to place on a hook or hanger designed for the purpose
6. _____ : to get (things) from different places and bring them together
7. _____ : to remove (something that is not wanted or needed)
8. _____ : to make a place completely clean and neat

Stop and Think! Who does most of the household chores in your country: men or women, adults or children? Does everyone share the work equally?

3 Cross out the words that don't work in each case.

1. Can you take this garbage / the car / these old bottles out please? Thanks!
2. Could someone wipe that dirt off the garden / tablecloth / window, please?
3. Are you going to clean the closet / cabinet / door out or not?
4. Could you hang your coat / shirt / sneakers up, please?
5. Put your books away in the chair / closet / drawer when you finish, OK?
6. I'm tired of picking your jeans / the cat / these shoes up off the floor!
7. Do you want to throw this garbage / laundry / old toothpaste away?
8. When you're free, can you help me clean up the living room / smartphone / yard?

5. wash off / up

6. put away / up

7. wipe away / off

8. clean down / out

Guess What!
Wash up is used in British English. In American English we say do the dishes.

Glossary

garbage: things you don't need and throw away

laundry: clothes that you wash and clean

Grammar

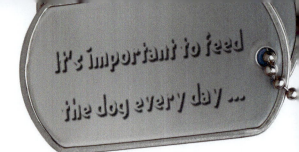

1 When you have a pet dog, what responsibilities do you have? Make a list.

2 Read Jesse's e-mail and number the pictures 1–3 in the order they are mentioned.

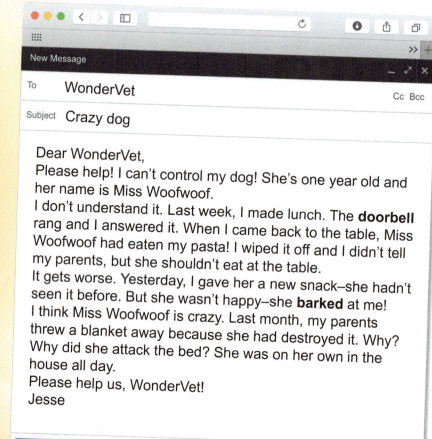

To: WonderVet
Subject: Crazy dog

Dear WonderVet,
Please help! I can't control my dog! She's one year old and her name is Miss Woofwoof.
I don't understand it. Last week, I made lunch. The **doorbell** rang and I answered it. When I came back to the table, Miss Woofwoof had eaten my pasta! I wiped it off and I didn't tell my parents, but she shouldn't eat at the table.
It gets worse. Yesterday, I gave her a new snack–she hadn't seen it before. But she wasn't happy–she **barked** at me!
I think Miss Woofwoof is crazy. Last month, my parents threw a blanket away because she had destroyed it. Why? Why did she attack the bed? She was on her own in the house all day.
Please help us, WonderVet!
Jesse

3 In pairs, discuss the questions. Then read WonderVet's reply to compare your answers.
Why do you think the dog behaves badly? Can you think of a solution?

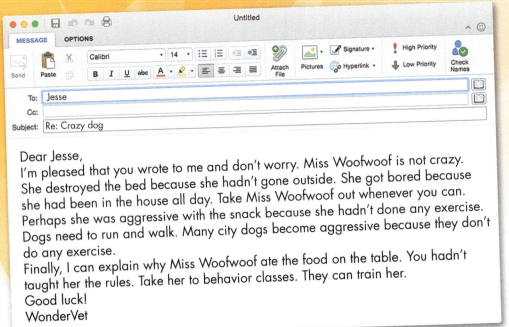

To: Jesse
Subject: Re: Crazy dog

Dear Jesse,
I'm pleased that you wrote to me and don't worry. Miss Woofwoof is not crazy. She destroyed the bed because she hadn't gone outside. She got bored because she had been in the house all day. Take Miss Woofwoof out whenever you can. Perhaps she was aggressive with the snack because she hadn't done any exercise. Dogs need to run and walk. Many city dogs become aggressive because they don't do any exercise.
Finally, I can explain why Miss Woofwoof ate the food on the table. You hadn't taught her the rules. Take her to behavior classes. They can train her.
Good luck!
WonderVet

Glossary
doorbell: this is outside your home. Visitors press it to make a noise to tell you that they are there
bark: the noise that a dog makes

 Stop and Think! Is it a good idea to keep a pet in an apartment in the city? Is it the same for a dog, a cat, a goldfish or a hamster?

4 Look at the sentences and answer the questions.

When I came back to the table, Miss Woofwoof had eaten my pasta!

Last month, my parents threw a blanket away because she had destroyed it.

1. Are these sentences in the present, past or future?
2. Look at the underlined verbs in each sentence. Which one happened first? Which one happened second? Number the actions in the order they happened.

The Past Perfect

Make the past perfect with had/ hadn't + past participle	You hadn't taught her the rules.
Use the past perfect with the past simple to describe an earlier past action.	She destroyed the bed because she hadn't gone outside.

 5 Think Fast! Underline four more examples of the past perfect in WonderVet's reply to Jesse.

6 Put the verb in parentheses in the past perfect.

1. Grandma thanked me because we _____
   (clean / the closet / out) for her.
2. My parents were angry because my little sister _____
   (not / put / her toys / away).
3. I couldn't find my favorite shirt because my mom _____
   (throw / it / away).
4. We _____
   (not / take / the trash / out) so the kitchen smelled horrible!
5. I wanted to write down the homework, but the teacher _____
   (wipe / it / off) the board.
6. Dad shouted at me because I _____
   (not / hang / my clothes up).

Listening & Speaking

> **Guess What!**
> On average, US mothers spend 18 hours on household chores every week. Fathers spend just 10 hours.

1 Discuss these questions.

1. How many brothers or sisters do you have?
2. Do you think it's better to come from a large family or a small family?
3. How do you distribute the chores in your family?

2 🎧12 Listen to Carlton describing the household chores in his family. Circle T (True) or F (False).

1. Carlton has four brothers and one sister.	T	F
2. Carlton is happy to come from a large family.	T	F
3. Carlton has his own bedroom.	T	F
4. Carlton does some chores every week.	T	F
5. Carlton's family has a special system to distribute the chores.	T	F
6. Carlton's parents pay him to do the chores.	T	F

3 🎧¹³ **The diagram shows how Carlton's family distributes the chores. Discuss how you think it works. Listen to check.**

4 **Listen again and complete the chores in each color of the wheel.**

5 **Think of all the chores that people do in your house: your parents, you and anybody else who lives with you. Put them in these groups.**

   1. Easy chores
   2. Disgusting chores
   3. Chores that take a long time
   4. Everyday chores
   5. Weekend chores

Be Strategic!
When listening for specific information, try not to write everything down. Write down key words only. For example, when you complete the wheel, just write down words like "bathroom," not "clean the bathroom."

6 **Work in groups of six. Imagine you live together. Design your own wheel with six names and six chores.**

   1. Choose six chores from Activity 5.
   2. Write your names on the wheel with six colors.
   3. Get a dice or six pieces of paper numbered 1–6. Distribute the chores for this week.
   4. Who is lucky or unlucky with the chores?
   5. If you don't want to do your chore, can you convince another member of the group to do it? What can you offer him/her?

Culture

THAILAND FACT FILE

1 🎧14 Complete the missing words in the fact file on Thailand. Then listen and check.

Thailand is a country in Southeast 1. _____. Its 2. _____ city is Bangkok. It has a population of about 68 3. _____ people. It is a hot country and it's very popular with tourists for its many beautiful 4. _____, such as the ones on the island of Koh Samui. The Thai 5. _____ is made of five stripes that are red, white and blue.

2 Read the text on the Songkran Festival in Thailand. Complete it with the missing sentences a–g (there is one extra).

a. People visit their grandparents and spend time together.
b. There are lots of these animals in Thailand.
c. It's a time to wipe off the dust and throw away all that garbage.
d. I had a spicy curry for lunch.
e. It lasts for two whole days.
f. Over there, it begins on April 13th.
g. They threw it all over me.

3 Work in pairs to answer the questions.

1. Where should you go to see the Songkran Festival?
2. When should you go?
3. What should you bring?
4. What should you wear?
5. What should you do?

4 Look at the pictures. Imagine the people below were at the Songkran Festival. In your notebook, write a comment for the blog on page 49 for each person. Were they happy or unhappy?

I was at the Songkran Festival last year …

Krit   Sudarat   Bob   Tamm

5 Discuss these questions.

1. Do you think a water festival like this would be a good idea in your hometown?
2. Where would you hold it?
3. When would you hold it?
4. How would you clean up after the festival?

Guess What!
The old name of Thailand was Siam. The adjective is still used today in some cases, for example, Siamese cats.

www.thailand.com

Getting Cleaned up in *Thailand!*

Spring cleaning is the time when we all clean up after the long winter. (1) ■ In other countries, it's a time for a fun celebration, like the Songkran Festival in Thailand.

Songkran is New Year in Southeast Asia. (2) ■ People begin the year with a special washing ceremony. People clean their homes from top to bottom. It's also a day to remember family. (3) ■

Other people have a more exciting way of celebrating Songkran. In the city of Chiang Mai in the north of the country, they have an enormous water fight. (4) ■ Over those 48 hours, everyone gets absolutely **soaked**!

I went there last year and I had never seen anything like it before. Everyone had a **water pistol** or a bowl of water. (5) ■ I had forgotten to bring dry clothes, so I went home wet from head to toe.

The most amazing thing was an elephant. (6) ■ People were laughing because it had covered them with water–from its **trunk**! It was funny, but a little disgusting. This is a cleaning festival, remember?!

Glossary
soaked: completely wet
water pistol: a toy gun that shoots water
trunk: an elephant's long nose

Project

 1 Think Fast! How many words do you know for members of the family? Can you think of one relative that begins with the letters F, M, B, S, D, G, C, N, U and A?

2 Families often argue. Think of one reason for an argument:

1. in the bathroom
2. in the living room
3. in the kitchen
4. in a shared bedroom
5. in the family car
6. about the laundry

3 🎧¹⁵ **Listen to the family. Answer the questions.**

1. Which picture is this? _____
2. What room are the people in? _____
3. How often does this situation happen? _____
4. Do they solve the problem? _____

4 🎧¹⁵ **Complete the conversation with the missing sentences a–e. Listen again to check.**

a. Can you come and help us, please?
b. Your mom told me she had asked you both to leave the remote in its place.
c. Where's the remote control?
d. I thought I had asked you to pick up your stuff.
e. Why can't you leave it in the same place?

DAD: Ryan! Madison! (1) ☐ I want to watch TV.

RYAN: I don't know.

MADISON: Last night, when I went to bed, Mom had left it in the living room.

DAD: It's not here! It should be on the coffee table! (2) ☐

MADISON: I'll help you look for it.

DAD: And look at the mess in this room! Comic books! Sweaters! (3) ☐

MADISON: Come on, Dad! I can't clean up all the time.

DAD: It's not here. This always happens! (4) ☐

MADISON: Ask Ryan. The last time you looked for it, he had left it in the kitchen.

DAD: Ryan! (5) ☐

RYAN: I'm busy, Dad! I'm doing my homework.

MADISON: I see it! It's on the fridge!

DAD: What? Who put it there?

MADISON: Hey, Dad, it's not my fault. Don't blame me!

DAD: This family is crazy!

5 **Perform the dialogue in Activity 4. One person is Dad, one person is Ryan and one person is Madison.**

6 **Work in small groups. Write a scene from a play.**

Step 1: Choose an argument at home. Think of a room and a common problem. Use your ideas from Activity 2 to help you.

Step 2: Choose your characters. They should all be family members.

Step 3: Write the play. Give everybody something to say. Use the dialogue in Activity 4 as a model.

Step 4: Perform your play for the rest of the class. If you have a smartphone, you can record it.

Review

1 Circle the correct option to complete the sentences.

1. Don't tell me you threw the newspaper _____! I hadn't finished it!
   a. up   b. away   c. on
2. We need to take the garbage _____. The bag's full.
   a. up   b. in   c. out
3. Hadn't I told you to hang your coat _____?
   a. up   b. down   c. away
4. I found this old photo while I was cleaning the closet _____.
   a. away   b. on   c. out
5. Playtime's over, kids. Put the toys _____.
   a. away   b. out   c. up
6. Nick, can you pick your room _____, please?
   a. away   b. up   c. on

2 🎧¹⁶ Listen and complete the conversation.

A: Honey, can you ¹_____ these clothes _____ please?
B: Sure mom. Err… Mom? Mom, why is my closet empty?
A: I ²_____ it _____ this afternoon.
B: You did what? Where is my comic book collection? It was in the closet.
A: Oh, I ³_____ those old comics _____ with the trash.
B: What? I had over a hundred comics in there! I'd collected them for years. I'm going to get them out of the trash can right now.
A: Ah, that will be difficult.
B: Why?
A: They ⁴_____ the trash _____ this afternoon.
B: How could you do this to me? My comic collection! Lost!
A: Don't blame me. I tell you to ⁵_____ your room _____ all the time and you never listen, so I did it.
B: My comic books are not trash!
A: They are now, dear. Now, help me ⁶_____ the hall _____ before your father comes home.
B: The hall? Who cares about the hall? This is the worst day of my entire life!

3 Match the statements to the responses. There are two extra responses.

1. It's impossible to find anything in this garage!
2. Quick! Masie's coming! Where can we hide her present?
3. I can't remember what color the carpet was in here.
4. Oh no! There's soda all over my keyboard!
5. These shoes are full of holes.
6. We should let the kids have a party every week.

a. I know. We really need to clean it out.
b. Relax. It's easy to wipe it off.
c. I hung them up in the closet.
d. It's time to throw them away.
e. I'll put it away in this drawer.
f. I get it, Dad. You're telling me to pick my room up, right?
g. I agree. It's the only time that they help clean up the house!
h. It's because we forgot to take the trash out last night.

4 Complete the sentences with the past perfect form of the verbs in parentheses.
1. Mom was angry because I _____ (not / wash) up the dishes.
2. Dom _____ (not / review) so he failed the exam.
3. We got to school late because we _____ (miss) the bus.
4. I _____ (have) a lot to eat, so I didn't have any dessert.
5. I lent Tim some money because he _____ (lost) his wallet.
6. They felt hungry because they _____ (not / eat) anything all day.

5 Circle the correct options to complete the text.

EXTREME IRONING

Some people thought that extreme ironing ¹**went / had gone** away, but now it has returned after 11 years! In 2015, Phil Shaw ²**returned / had returned** to the sport that he had invented the 1990s to introduce a while new audience to the craziest hobby on earth.

So what is extreme ironing? Basically, it's doing this household chore in incredible situations. Phil originally did the ironing up a mountain after he ³**found / had found** a big pile of laundry at home. Soon other people ⁴**copy / copied** him and they came up with even more extreme ideas. One Australian did his ironing wearing a parachute after he ⁵**jumped / had jumped** off one of the Blue Mountains near Sydney. Another even did the ironing underwater, although he clearly ⁶**didn't wait / hadn't waited** for the clothes to dry before he started!

6 Correct the sentences.
1. Neil will go to the dentist because he had lost a tooth.
_____
2. It hadn't rained for months, so all the plants in the garden die.
_____
3. We go to the supermarket because there wasn't any food in the fridge.
_____
4. I fell asleep in class because I will sleep the night before.
_____
5. We will have a problem in the bathroom and there was water everywhere!
_____

Just for Fun

1 Follow the lines to find out each person's chore. There is one person who doesn't have any chores this week.

2 Read the parts of a joke and number them in the correct sequence.

☐ The cowboy got back on his horse. The barman went up to him and asked in a nervous voice, "Uh before you go, please tell us, what exactly happened in Texas?" "I had to walk home," said the cowboy.

☐ The other customers in the bar looked at each other and shivered–they were terrified. When the cowboy had finished his second drink, he went back outside. The thief had brought the horse back and tied it to a post.

☐ "OK, then, I'll tell you what I'm going to do. I'm going to order myself another drink. I'm going to drink it and then I'm going to go back outside. If my horse isn't back where I left him, I'll have to do what I did when the same thing happened in Texas."

☐ "Which one of you stole my horse?", he shouted, and then he fired three more shots into the bottles behind the bar.

☐ A cowboy rode into a town. He fastened his big fine horse to a post outside a bar, kicked open the door, walked up to the bar and asked for a drink. When he had finished it, he went back outside. He went back into the bar, got his gun out and fired three shots into the ceiling.

3 Match the two halves to make nationality adjectives. Think of five more nationality adjectives.

Fre Th Sw Span Peru Pakistan Du Chil Gre Iceland Colomb Mexi

vian i nch tch iss can ian ic ai ean ish ek

Vocabulary

1 Look at the pictures on pages 56 and 57. Write the correct numbers.

a. fortune cat ☐
b. horseshoe ☐
c. four-leaf clover ☐
d. evil eye ☐
e. rabbit's foot ☐
f. fortune cookies ☐
g. ladybug ☐

2 Read and write the correct number that describes each picture.

1. I won tickets to see a movie premier — but I **stupidly** left them in my jeans and they went in the washing machine!
2. I once wrote an angry text message about my best friend —and then I **accidentally** sent it to to her!
3. I broke a **mirror noisily** at a friend's house. I'm going to have seven years of bad luck!
4. I saw a black cat crossing the street and we played **badly** the whole season!
5. I saw a four-leaf clover while I was jogging. I jogged **slowly** to get a better look.

Glossary
mirror: a piece of glass that reflects images
fly away: to cause to fly

3 Match the underlined words in Activity 2 with their opposites.

1. well _____
2. quickly _____
3. cleverly _____
4. silently _____
5. deliberately _____

4 🎧¹⁷ Complete the sentences with the words from Activity 3. Then listen and check.

1. One day, I saw a ladybug. I went toward it _____ so it didn't fly away and I took an amazing photo! The best of my life.
2. We won the school music competition! We practiced for months and we played really _____.
3. My sister says I _____ broke her laptop, but I didn't! It was an accident! I spilled some soda.
4. We saw the bus and ran _____ down the street and I fell down and broke my nose. It's the third time, so my sister gave me a rabbit's foot for good luck.
5. My grades are low in English class. I _____ studied as much as I could and I got a better grade!

5 In pairs, read the sentences in Activities 2 and 4 again. Discuss which ones are accidents or related to the person's luck or effort.

Stop and Think! Do we make our own luck? Is it by effort or by accident?

6 **Think Fast!** We make many adverbs by adding –ly to a verb, for example, *quick → quickly, happy → happily*. How many other adverbs can you make?

2 min

Grammar

1 Look at the pictures with a partner. Discuss which ones are good or bad luck.

2 🎧¹⁸ Listen and number the pictures in the order you hear them.

3 🎧¹⁸ Listen again and complete the sentences.

1. If I _____ Leo Messi, I wouldn't be able to say anything. I'd feel really shy.
2. I wouldn't _____ this message if it appeared on my screen and I certainly wouldn't click on any link.
3. If someone stole my bag, I'd _____ an adult for help. I wouldn't run after the thief because it would be dangerous.
4. If I _____ the Loch Ness Monster, I would definitely take a photo of it!
5. If I _____ $100 in the street, I wouldn't take it.
6. If a snail fell out of my bag of salad, I'd _____ it and eat it anyway.

The Second Conditional

If I **lived** in Hawaii, I **would go** to the beach every day.
(verb in past simple)   (would + verb in the base form)

I **wouldn't be** happy if I **were** a famous rock star.
(would + not + verb in the base form)   (verb in past simple)

Guess What!
We use a comma in the first part of the sentence when it starts with *if*.

4 Look at the sentences in Activity 3 and answer the questions.
1. Are the sentences describing real or hypothetical events?
2. What verb do we use in the *if* part of the sentence?
3. What verb do we use in the second part of the sentence?

5 Match the sentence halves.

1. If someone **spilled** ketchup all over my clothes,
2. If I won $1,000,000,
3. If a **genie** gave me one **wish**,
4. If I broke a mirror,
5. If I lost my smart phone,
6. If I won a competition to travel anywhere in the world,

a. I'd have seven years of bad luck.
b. I'd go to Antarctica.
c. I'd laugh about it because it would be an accident.
d. I'd use a pay phone to call my parents.
e. I'd ask him to make me taller.
f. I'd give it to my parents.

6 In your notebook, change the sentences in Activity 5 so they are true for you.

7 Use the prompts to make second conditional sentences. Then compare with a partner.

1. win a ticket / see / my favorite band
2. lose / my tablet
3. my favorite singer / sign autograph
4. friend / give / my favorite video game
5. fortune cookie message / say / be lucky

Glossary
spill: to accidentally drop a liquid on something
genie: a magic creature from Arabia that lives in a lamp
a wish: a desire for something that is usually impossible

Reading & Writing

1 Read Molly's e-mail and answer the questions.
1. What is Molly's hobby?
2. What is her problem?
3. Why is she writing the e-mail?
4. Is it a formal or an informal e-mail?

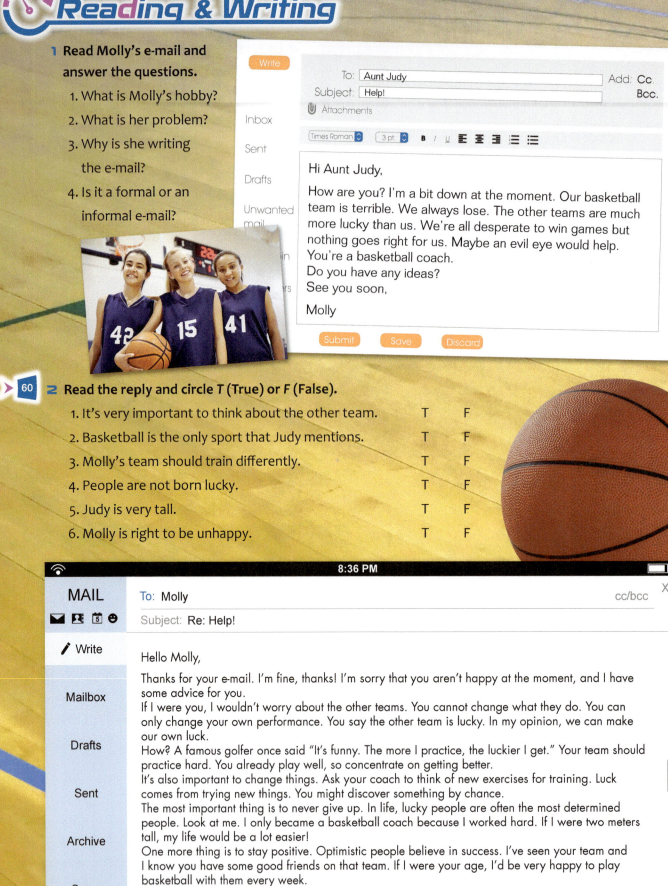

To: Aunt Judy
Subject: Help!

Hi Aunt Judy,

How are you? I'm a bit down at the moment. Our basketball team is terrible. We always lose. The other teams are much more lucky than us. We're all desperate to win games but nothing goes right for us. Maybe an evil eye would help. You're a basketball coach.
Do you have any ideas?
See you soon,

Molly

2 Read the reply and circle *T* (True) or *F* (False).
1. It's very important to think about the other team.   T   F
2. Basketball is the only sport that Judy mentions.   T   F
3. Molly's team should train differently.   T   F
4. People are not born lucky.   T   F
5. Judy is very tall.   T   F
6. Molly is right to be unhappy.   T   F

MAIL

To: Molly
Subject: Re: Help!

Hello Molly,

Thanks for your e-mail. I'm fine, thanks! I'm sorry that you aren't happy at the moment, and I have some advice for you.
If I were you, I wouldn't worry about the other teams. You cannot change what they do. You can only change your own performance. You say the other team is lucky. In my opinion, we can make our own luck.
How? A famous golfer once said "It's funny. The more I practice, the luckier I get." Your team should practice hard. You already play well, so concentrate on getting better.
It's also important to change things. Ask your coach to think of new exercises for training. Luck comes from trying new things. You might discover something by chance.
The most important thing is to never give up. In life, lucky people are often the most determined people. Look at me. I only became a basketball coach because I worked hard. If I were two meters tall, my life would be a lot easier!
One more thing is to stay positive. Optimistic people believe in success. I've seen your team and I know you have some good friends on that team. If I were your age, I'd be very happy to play basketball with them every week.

Love to your mom and dad!
Speak soon,

Judy

3 Look again at Aunt Judy's e-mail. Write four suggestions that she makes.
1. _____
2. _____
3. _____
4. _____

4 Read Molly and Judy's e-mails again. Write the following information.
1. A friendly way to start an e-mail. _____
2. A way of asking and answering about someone's health. _____
3. An example of a contraction. _____
4. A friendly way to end an e-mail. _____

Be Strategic!
When writing, it is important to be aware of your reader. In a formal e-mail, you begin with "Dear" and end with a phrase like "Best wishes" or "Best regards."
In an informal e-mail, begin with "Hi" or "Hello" and end with "See you soon" or "Bye for now."
We also use contractions in informal writing ("I'm" or "we're"), but not in formal writing.

5 Read Logan's e-mail. In your notebook, write him an reply. Give him some advice.

snt05.mail.live.com

4:30 PM

To: Tammy
Subject: Not again!

Hi Tammy,
I'm so unlucky. My mom has to move a lot in her job and I often change schools. I was just happy in my last middle school, but now we're moving again.
My middle school now is in Tampa, Florida. My new school will be in Portland, Oregon. It's hundreds of miles away and there's a time difference. When it's 10 a.m. in Florida, it's 7 a.m. in Oregon.
I'll **miss** all my friends and I don't know anyone in my new school. It's a **nightmare**! What would you do if you were in my position?

Logan

00485MG.jpg

Glossary
miss (someone): feel unhappy because someone is not with you
nightmare: a terrible experience / a bad dream

> ⏱ 3 min **1 Think Fast!** Name as many gods as you can. You could choose gods from any mythology (Roman, Greek, Aztec, etc.). Hint: think of the names of planets.

2 Read the short history of the Roman Empire. Then answer the questions.

1. What was the religion in the beginning?
2. What was the religion at the end?

Rome

The Roman Empire was enormous. In 117 AD, it went as north as Scotland and as south as Egypt. At the center was the capital city, Rome.

People in Ancient Rome worshipped many gods. The king of the Gods was Jupiter and his queen was Juno. There was also the god of the Sun, Apollo, and the goddess of love, Venus.

The Romans worshipped real people, too. After his death in 44 BC, the famous general Julius Caesar "became" a god! Later, Rome changed. Christianity became popular and in 380 AD, it finally became the official religion of the empire and people forgot the old gods.

3 Read the text in Activity 2 again. Make a list of the gods mentioned.

4 🎧19 Complete the text with the missing sentences. There is one extra. Then listen to check your answers.

a. Many of these gods originally came from Ancient Greece.
b. After he died, they built temples in his memory.
c. People still talk about "Lady Luck" today.
d. One looks back into the past and one looks into the future.

Strange Gods of Rome

Fortuna was the goddess of luck. (1) ☐. There is often a piece of material over her eyes. This is because luck is **blind**. She also has the wheel of fortune. The wheel moves. When you are on top, you are lucky and happy. When you are at the bottom, you are unlucky and very unhappy!

Janus was the god of the beginning and the end. He has two faces. (2) ☐. The month January gets its name from this god because it is the end of one year and the beginning of the next.

Like Julius Caesar, Augustus was a real person, but the Romans **worshipped** him like a god. He was emperor for a long time 27 BC–14 AD (41 years). (3) ☐. The Romans named our modern month August after him, and they named July after Julius Caesar.

5 Label the pictures with the correct names of the gods in Activity 4.

Stop and Think! How are good and bad luck represented in your country? Is there a symbol for each one? Are they different from other countries?

6 Look at the picture of the god Atlas. Discuss the questions with a partner.
1. What is he doing?
2. How do we use his name today?
3. Why do we use his name for a modern atlas?

7 🎧²⁰ Listen and check your answers.

Glossary
blind: unable to see
worship: to show your respect in a religion

Project

1 Read the dictionary definitions. Discuss common superstitions in your country with a partner.

superstition – *noun* something that people believe will give them good luck or bad luck. They have no scientific or logical reason for thinking like this.

superstitious – *adj* a person who believes in superstitions

2 🎧²¹ Look at the poster of a popular superstition. Listen and complete the sentences.

Superstitions Around the World
#1 Black Cats

> **Guess What!**
> The hashtag # is not just for tweets. It also means number in American English: #14 = number fourteen

Black cats bring (1) _____ good luck and bad luck, depending on the country!

Stop and Think! In many countries, people think Friday the 13th is unlucky. Is this true in your country?

All over Europe, people think black cats bring bad luck, especially in (2) _____.

The cruel superstitions about black cats cause problems today. Many people don't want a black cat as a (6) _____.
Some 70% of cats without a home are black cats.

64

It's because black cats often accompany **witches** in old stories. People saw cats as symbols of black (3) _____.

Cats are also good luck in (5) _____. If a black cat walks across your path, you can control your own luck!

The exception is Britain. In Scotland, people think black cats are lucky, especially when one comes to your (4) _____.

3 Read the poster again. Circle T (True) or F (False).

1. English people think cats bring good luck when they come into your house. T F
2. Black cats bring bad luck everywhere. T F
3. Black cats bring good luck in Asia. T F
4. Many people still don't like black cats. T F
5. The author of the poster doesn't like some of the superstitions. T F

4 Work in small groups. Create a poster for "Superstitions Around the World."

Step 1: Choose a superstition relating to good luck or bad luck. Look back through the superstitions in this unit or think of one from your country. Choose a superstition that is easy to illustrate.

Step 2: Research your superstition on the Internet (if possible). Why is it good or bad luck? Where does the superstition come from? What countries have this superstition?

Step 3: Plan your poster. Think of how to communicate the idea as simply as possible. Think of the information it contains. Is all the information necessary?

Step 4: Create your poster. Place the posters on the classroom wall.

Step 5: Read the posters from the other groups. Which is the strangest superstition?

 Glossary
witch: an evil woman who uses black magic

Review

1 Find ten adverbs in the word search.

```
A N G R I L Y X H G
N I C E L Y Q W A X
Z B J G W P T L P N
D K T U M Z K A P O
N E W L Y H K Z I I
Q Q G A S J R I L S
W S T R O N G L Y I
U X X L Z W Q Y J L
J U K Y S A D L Y Y
Z S U D D E N L Y X
```

2 Complete the sentences with the adverb form of the adjective in parentheses.

1. I _____ (accidental) fell off my skateboard! I woke up on the wrong side of the bed!
2. My brother plays basketball really _____ (bad).
3. We _____ (quick) finished our homework.
4. You _____ (deliberate) broke my pen. I know you did!
5. Grandma's 80 years old, so she walks _____ (slow).

3 Cross out the wrong word in each sentence.

1. They talked **noisily / quickly / accidentally** during the conference.
2. I **deliberately / stupidly / newly** threw my old sneakers away.
3. My computer is working **accidentally / badly / slowly** today and I have homework!
4. I speak **badly / cleverly / slowly** in German because it's not my first language.
5. Dad was asleep on the sofa, so we walked very **noisily / silently / slowly** across the living room.
6. I needed some facts for my essay and it was impossible to find them, but I **cleverly / slowly / stupidly** found them after a careful Internet search.
7. Xavi is walking **badly / quickly / slowly** because he has hurt his leg. He was very unlucky.
8. I couldn't do my computer project, so I **badly / cleverly / quickly** asked my cousin for help. She's a programmer!

4 Write sentences to describe each picture. Use adverbs from Activity 3.

1. _____
2. _____
3. _____

5 **Match the sentence halves.**
   1. If I were a mermaid,
   2. I would immediately buy a lottery ticket
   3. My neighborhood would be a great place to live
   4. You would have your own bedroom
   5. If I gave my parents a fortune cat,
   6. If you played a musical instrument,

   a. if I found a four-leaf clover.
   b. we would invite you to join our band.
   c. if your sister went to college.
   d. I would swim all around the world.
   e. they would sell more in their store.
   f. if it had a swimming pool.

6 **Complete the sentences with the correct form of the words in parentheses. Then listen and check.**

   MADISON: If I were a famous actor, I (1) _____ (be) so happy! What a life!
   DYLAN: What a life? You (2) _____ (get) really stressed if you were famous.
   MADISON: Why?
   DYLAN: Every time you left your house, photographers (3) _____ (take) your photo. If you (4) _____ (go) to the store, people would follow you everywhere.
   MADISON: If I (5) _____ (wear) a hat and sunglasses, nobody would recognize me.
   DYLAN: You can't wear sunglasses all the time! If you lived in the same house as now, you (6) _____ (not / have) any privacy. If anyone (7) _____ (see) you in the street, they would ask for a selfie. Imagine thousands of people around you with their smartphones.
   MADISON: What are you saying, Dylan?
   DYLAN: You (8) _____ (not / enjoy) life if you were famous. It's a dream. It's not real life.
   MADISON: Speak for yourself! Luck is on my side and I want to be a star!

7 **Complete the sentences about you.**
   1. If I were my parents, _____.
   2. If I walked under a ladder, _____.
   3. If I didn't have to go to school, _____.
   4. If a friend gave me a good luck charm, _____.
   5. If I had another brother or sister, _____.
   6. If I went skydiving, _____.

Just for Fun

1 Read and write the number that describes each lucky charm.

1. This number is lucky in China because it sounds like the word for "wealth," which means "having a lot of money."
2. The aborigine people of Australia believed that frogs bring good luck. Because they live in water, frogs bring rain to the land, something very important in Australia's deserts.
3. People in England always kiss a fish before they cook it to say sorry for taking it out of the river or the sea. If you forget to do this, you will never catch a fish again.
4. A pig is very good luck in Germany. In the old days, people with a lot of money had a lot of pigs, so they represented good fortune. Germans still give pigs as presents at New Year.

2 One of the lucky charms in Activity 1 is false. Guess which one.

3 In your notebook, answer these questions so they are true for you. Then compare with a partner.

1. If you had a time machine, would you go forward to the future or back into the past? Where and when would you go?

2. If you found a magic lamp and a genie gave you one wish, what would it be?

3. If you were able to meet a fictional character, who would you choose?

4. If you had a superpower, what would it be?

5. If they made a movie of your life, which actor would play you?

6. If you were King or Queen for a day, what laws would you change?

Vocabulary

1 Number the pictures.
1. boarding pass
2. customs
3. luggage (suitcases)
4. passport
5. visa stamps

a

b

c

d

e

2 🎧²³ Look at the stages of traveling by plane. Number them in the order they happen. Then listen and check.

☐ You book your flights.

☐ You check in your luggage.

☐ You pick up your suitcases at baggage claim.

☐ You board the plane.

☐ The plane takes off.

☐ You land at your destination.

☐ You print out your boarding pass.

☐ You go through customs.

☐ You arrive at the airport.

☐ You go through passport control.

3 Close your books. Write down in order the stages of traveling by plane.

Guess What! The longest nonstop flight in the world is 13,800 kilometers long between Dubai and Panama City. It takes 17 and a half hours!

Stop and Think! Do you need a visa to go to the US or anywhere else? What are the steps to get a visa?

70

Pictures

4 🎧²⁴ Complete the messages with the words in the box. Then listen and check.

bridge   mosque   pyramid   ruins   stadium   statues   temple   wall

create album   add photos   add videos

This is the Great (5) _____ of China. It's a dream to be here!

Rapa Nui's mysterious *moai* (2) _____ stand on Easter Island.

I'm at the Colosseum in Rome. It's an ancient sports (3) _____ where people watched races and fights.

This is the great (4) _____ of Giza in Egypt. It was once the tallest structure on Earth!

This building is a (1) _____ at Angkor Wat in Cambodia. It's awesome!

The Blue (6) _____ in Turkey is one of the most important buildings in Islam.

These are the (7) _____ of the ancient city of Machu Picchu in Peru. What a place!

The Ponte Vecchio is the most beautiful (8) _____ in Florence, Italy. What a way to cross a river!

5 In your notebook, make a list of places like the ones in Activity 4 that are in your country. Are they easy to visit?

6 Think Fast! In your notebook, write down as many types of building as you can, e.g., supermarket. (3 min)

7 Imagine you traveled by plane to one of the places in Activity 4. Write a post for your friends at home. Include the information below.
1. What you needed from Activity 1.
2. What you are doing.
3. How you feel.
4. A fun punch line.

71

How brave a traveler are you?

1 Answer the quiz and check your answers. Then compare with a partner.

You're staying in a foreign country for the first time. What would you do in these situations? Are you a tourist, a traveler or an adventurer?

1 You are staying in a foreign country. Would you prefer...
   a. ○ to travel through the jungle to look at an ancient temple?
   b. ○ to go to the city museum and look at ancient statues?
   c. ○ to take a guided tour on a tour bus?

2 It's dinner time. Would you like...
   a. ○ to eat everything and anything from the local country?
   b. ○ to try a few local dishes in a restaurant?
   c. ○ to eat in fast food restaurants, just like at home?

3 Now you have some free time. Would you rather...
   a. ○ do a bungee jump off the country's biggest bridge?
   b. ○ go cycling along the old city walls?
   c. ○ read a book next to the hotel pool?

4 People in the country speak a different language. Would you prefer...
   a. ○ to learn some of the local language to be polite?
   b. ○ to speak English to everyone?
   c. ○ not to say anything so you don't embarrass yourself?

5 You're in a country that's famous for its wildlife. Would you rather...
   a. ○ go swimming with sharks?
   b. ○ visit the city zoo?
   c. ○ not see any of the local animals?

6 You want to buy a souvenir for your family back home. Would you like...
   a. ○ to buy a little handmade statue from a local artist?
   b. ○ to buy a model of a local building like the pyramids?
   c. ○ to buy a box of chocolates in the airport before you board your plane?

Answers

Mostly A: Wow! You are an adventurer. Every time you go on vacation, you probably discover some ancient ruins.
Mostly B: You are a sensible traveler. You like a bit of adventure, but most of the time, you play it safe.
Mostly C: You are a nervous traveler. You should stop worrying and have a bit of fun. Nothing in this world is 100% safe.

Preferences

I would like to stay in that hotel.
I wouldn't like to stay in that hotel.

I'd prefer to eat in a restaurant.
I'd prefer not to eat in a restaurant.

I'd rather stay at home today.
I'd rather not stay at home today.

2 Circle the correct options to complete the sentences.
1. She'd rather **not** / **no** go to the mall. She doesn't like window shopping.
2. I'd prefer **share** / **to share** a hotel room with my sister.
3. I **wouldn't like to** / **wouldn't like** be on a plane for 10 hours.
4. They'd rather **to have** / **have** spaghetti than fish.
5. Would you prefer **go** / **to go** to the movies or the park?

3 Complete the sentences so they are true for you. Then compare with a partner.
1. I'd rather _____ than pick up my room.
2. I'd prefer to _____ than go to school on Saturday.
3. I'd rather not _____ on Friday night.
4. I'd like to _____ at some point this year.
5. I wouldn't like to _____ on holiday.

4 🎧²⁵ Listen to the conversation. Circle T (True) or F (False).
1. Chase is going on vacation.   T   F
2. Chase's mom packed his suitcase.   T   F
3. His suitcase is very heavy.   T   F
4. Chase is an adventurous traveler.   T   F

5 🎧²⁵ Listen again and complete the sentences in the box.

Too and Enough

Use *too* when there is an excess of something.
Use *enough* to mean "sufficient."
1. These bags are too _____.
2. I'm not _____ enough to pick this suitcase up.

6 Unscramble the sentences.
1. don't have / for / I / money / a new bike / enough
   _____
2. for me / difficult / pronunciation / too / Spanish / is
   _____
3. to go / I / time / today / have / enough / mall / to the
   _____
4. old / any movie / enough / I'm / to see / at the theater
   _____
5. is / my journey / to school / long / too
   _____

7 In your notebook, change the sentences in Activity 6 so they are true for you.

1 🎧²⁶ **Listen and number the pictures.**

2 🎧²⁶ **Complete the story with the correct words. Then listen again to check.**

Last summer, my friend Chelsea had (1) _____ on vacation with her parents on a cruise through the Pacific. On the fourth night, she couldn't sleep and she decided to go for a walk.

On the main deck, she didn't see a lot of people. There was a man admiring the stars with a telescope. There was a couple (2) _____ near the flag pole. They were kissing. Chelsea blushed, turned around and began walking to the other side of the main deck.

Suddenly, she saw someone, or at least a shadow, jumping into the ocean. She screamed and immediately a crewman arrived and asked her if she was OK. "Someone (3) _____ just jumped off the board, hurry, he might be still alive!" said Chelsea. The crewman asked her if she was sure about that. "Yes! Well, I saw a shadow." The crewman reported the incident to the captain. Some crewmen looked for any evidence that indicated that someone had (4) _____ the ship, but they found nothing. Not knowing what else to do, Chelsea went back to her cabin and fell asleep. The next morning, Chelsea woke up and wondered if everything (5) _____ been a bad dream. She got up and went to look for her parents to have breakfast. On her way to the dining room she saw the captain talking to some crewmen. They looked very concerned. Chelsea (6) _____ a chill all over her body...

74

Be Strategic!
When you write a narrative, use different past forms.
Use the past simple for the main events of the story.
Use the past continuous for background information (*One night, it was raining and…*).
Use the past perfect for events which happened before other past events (*While I was out of my room someone had stolen my smartphone!*)

3 Read the story in Activity 2 again. Find two examples of each tense.

1. The Past Simple
2. The Past Continuous
3. The Past Perfect

 Stop and Think! Many people say "it was all a dream" is a bad ending to a story. Do you agree? Why? Why not?

4 In pairs, read the definition of Flash Fiction. In your notebooks, write the setting, characters and plot of the story in Activity 2. Discuss the ending of the story.

Flash Fiction

Flash fiction is a popular way of writing mostly on the Internet. It is a short story. A piece of flash fiction is 150–1000 words long. Flash fiction can be any genre: drama, crime, romance or science-fiction. It has the elements of a story–**setting**, characters, **plot** and ending.

5 Work in small groups. In your notebook, write your piece of Flash Fiction (150 words). Read the guidelines below.

1. Include one of these places in your story: bridge, ruins, stadium or street.
2. Think about your main character. Who is he / she? How old is he / she?
3. What was the weather like at the beginning of your story? Was it raining / snowing / windy / sunny?
4. Use different tenses: the past simple, the past continuous and the past perfect.
5. Think of a "catch," a clever ending to the story.

6 Exchange your story with other groups. Which story was the most interesting? Why?

Glossary
setting: the place and conditions in which a story happens
plot: the problem or conflict in a story

Culture

1 Read about a way to travel through Europe.

People in Europe can buy an Interrail Pass. This allows them to travel on trains around Europe. The Interrail Pass covers more than 30 countries and it's much cheaper than paying for normal train tickets. You travel by train and you can also take ferries to cross the sea where necessary. The trains are modern and they go through some amazing countryside, like the mountains of the Swiss Alps. If you don't have enough time, you can also travel on a sleeper train and spend the night on board. You share a **carriage** on the train and sleep in **bunk beds**. You have to pay extra to do this, but the price is not too expensive. It's an exciting and easy way for young people to travel around Europe. It's a backpacker's dream!

Trains in Europe

High-speed trains
Alvia
Spanish Alvia high-speed trains can go as fast as 250 km/h. They connect major cities across Spain and offer modern comforts, such as spacious reclining seats, fold-away tables, as well as audio and video outlets.

Night trains
EN Austria-Italy
Cover large distances as you sleep. The EuroNight Austria-Italy connects Vienna with Italian cities like Rome, Milan and Venice. There are four trains running each night.

Dublin, Harwich, London, Amsterdam, Rotterdam, Brussels, Berlin, Paris, Munich, Milan, Lisbon, Madrid, Barcelona, Rome

Guess What!
Before the euro appeared in 2002, every country in Europe had a different currency. Germany used *marks*, France used *francs*, Italy used *lira*, etc.

Regional trains

Regional trains can take you everywhere– from the smallest villages to the continent's busiest capital cities. If you are traveling on a budget, most regional trains don't require any reservations.

Scenic trains

Bernina Express
The Bernina Express is an amazing train ride through the snow-capped mountain scenery of Switzerland. Get views of glaciers, alpine lakes and rolling countryside.

Thessaloniki

Athens

2 Read the clues and solve the crossword.

(Crossword with answer INTERRAIL running down)

1. Some trains offer _____ facilities like spacious seats.
2. Alvia trains are very _____.
3. It's more _____ to buy normal tickets.
4. The _____ is the money you're planning to spend on a trip.
5. The Alps are a beautiful natural _____.
6. In the EN Austria-Italy trains you can _____ at night.
7. The trains _____ you with most countries in Europe.
8. You can take a _____ to cross the sea.
9. _____ trains operate significantly faster than traditional ones.

3 🎧27 Listen to two friends preparing for their Interrail trip. Mark (✓) the places they mention.

- [ ] A bridge
- [ ] A park
- [ ] An airport
- [ ] A market
- [ ] A stadium
- [ ] Pyramids
- [ ] A mosque
- [ ] A temple
- [ ] Ruins
- [ ] A museum
- [ ] A wall

4 🎧27 Listen again. Trace their route on the map.

5 Think Fast! Name the ten countries where the cities on the map are located.
(2 min)

Glossary
carriage: one separate part of a train
bunk beds: beds where one person sleeps in a bed above another one

Project

 1 Think Fast! Make a list of the most common places of tourist accommodation.

2 Choose a destination you would like to visit. Mark (✓) the information you need to know before your trip.

	I really need to know this	I'd like to know this	This is useful but not essential	I wouldn't look up this information before my trip
1. How do I get there?				
2. Is the hotel nice?				
3. What is the food like?				
4. Are there fun sports activities?				
5. What is there to do in the evening?				
6. Is it dangerous?				

3 Number the texts with the questions in Activity 2.

tripadvisor

a. ☐ The sun is intense in August and it is too hot to go the beach between 11a.m. and 3 in the afternoon. It is also very humid, so it is not the best time to do physical excursions, such as hiking.

b.  ☐ As a beach resort, we are next to the sea and fish is a big part of our diet. Sea urchins are particularly popular.

d. 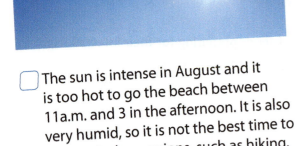 ☐ The resort is an island, so the only way to arrive is by ferry or plane. There is a major international airport with several flights a day. All visitors require a visa, but you can get it in your passport on arrival.

e.  ☐ Visitors aged 12–16 usually go to the mini-disco which runs from 8 to 10 p.m. The music is all rock and pop. Kids who aren't old enough to go to the disco can play in our games room, where board games and computer games are available

4 Discuss the reasons why you would prefer or would rather not go to the resort in Activity 3 with a partner.

5 Think of the destination you chose in Activity 2. In small groups, write a guide for travelers like the one in Activity 3. Use the Internet to research your ideas. Use these ideas to help you:
- choose a specific place like a city, town or a beach. Don't choose a country because this area is too big.
- choose a place that is popular with tourists. You need a place that has enough activities and places to go out.
- what kind of accommodation is there? Look up information on the Internet using terms like "camping in Orlando" or "youth hostels in the Grand Canyon."
- find one typical dish in the area to describe.
- use websites like Tripadvisor® to find out how people rate your destination.

6 Exchange your guide with another group. Imagine you're spending one day together in the place suggested. Discuss and agree on what to do that day.

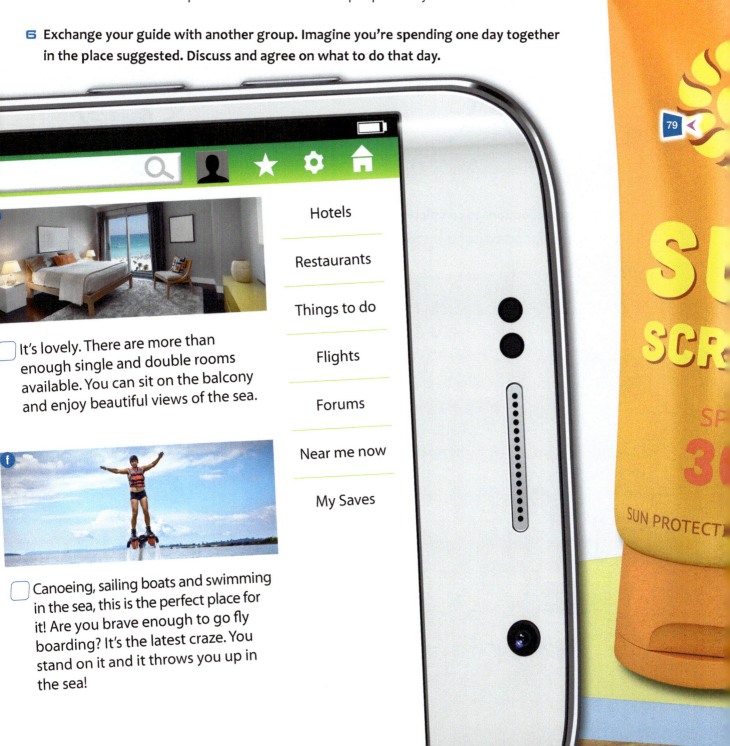

It's lovely. There are more than enough single and double rooms available. You can sit on the balcony and enjoy beautiful views of the sea.

Canoeing, sailing boats and swimming in the sea, this is the perfect place for it! Are you brave enough to go fly boarding? It's the latest craze. You stand on it and it throws you up in the sea!

Review

1 Follow and write the words for air travel.

2 Circle the correct options to complete the sentences.

1. We're **arriving** / **boarding** the plane at Gate 41.
2. Let's go to baggage claim to **check in** / **pick up** our luggage.
3. We should get to the airport two hours before our flight **lands** / **takes off**.
4. I only have hand luggage, so I don't have to **check in** / **print out** any bags.
5. Our plane is delayed. It won't **land** / **take off** for another hour.
6. You can **board** / **book** flights to Montevideo on this website.
7. Everybody has to **go through** / **pick up** customs when they arrive.
8. The boarding passes have arrived in my e-mail. I'll just **check them in** / **print them out** now.

3 Look at the icons and write the places. What is the mystery word?

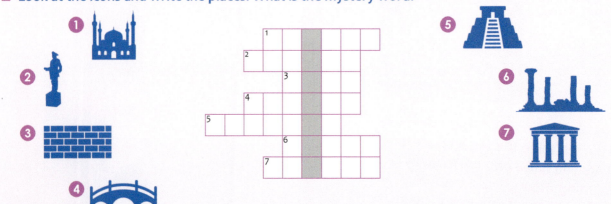

Owl Wood Adventure Park

4 Complete the posts with the words in the boxes. There's one extra in each post.

How was your trip to the Owl Wood Adventure Park? Write your comments below!

Sebastian 😊😊😊😊😊

> mosque   pyramids   stadium   wall

It was so cool! We stayed three nights at the park and we slept in rooms that were like (1) _____! They looked like ancient Egyptian structures. We also did sports every day. I loved climbing a (2) _____. You have to go right up to the top. It was 10 meters high! There is also a (3)_____ where we played soccer and baseball. Our team won every game. It was a very cool trip!

Savannah 😊😊😊

> bridge   ruins   statue   temple

It was OK. I liked the adventure sports best. We walked over this (4) _____ of wood and ropes. It was awesome. Unfortunately, I was with my parents. They took this embarrassing photo of me next to a (5) _____ in front of all my friends. Not cool. We also did a game where you explore these old (6) _____ with lots of columns and rocks. Lots of teams had to find the treasure and we came in second.

5 Complete the conversations with the correct form of the verbs in parentheses.

1. **A:** Do you want to go to the mall or the movies?
   B: I'd prefer _____ (*go*) to the mall.
2. **A:** Everyone has to cook or wash the dishes on the camping trip.
   B: I'd rather _____ (*wash*) the dishes because I'm not a good cook.
3. **A:** Do you have any ideas for the weekend?
   B: I'd like _____ (*play*) tennis.
4. **A:** I'm going to wear jeans on the trip to the jungle.
   B: I'd prefer _____ (*wear*) shorts because it'll be really hot.
5. **A:** Look at this! This tent is on the side of a mountain!
   B: I wouldn't like _____ (*sleep*) in one of those.

6 Complete the sentences with *too* or *enough*.

1. My brother is _____ young to fly on his own.
2. I'm old _____ to go on a train journey on my own.
3. A youth hostel is good _____ for me. I don't need to stay in a five-star hotel!
4. Oh no! We missed the train! We're _____ late!
5. We can't go on vacation this year. We don't have _____ money.

Just for Fun

1 Look at the picture for thirty seconds. Then close your books. Name as many objects as possible.

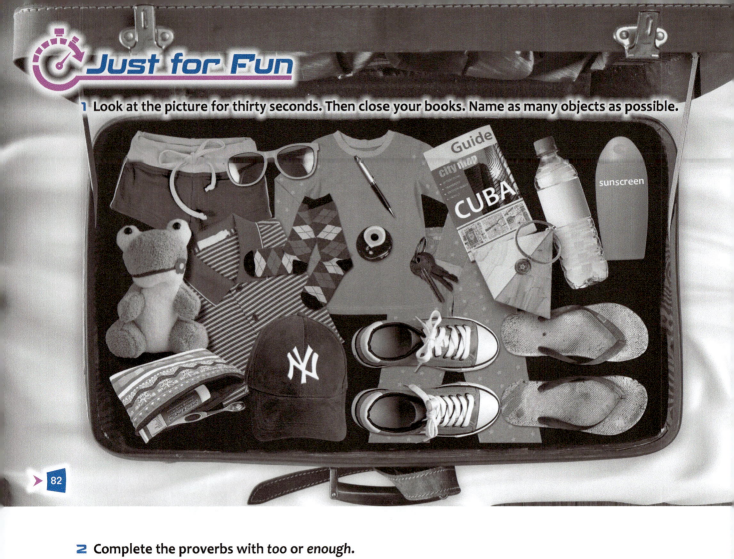

2 Complete the proverbs with *too* or *enough*.

1. _____ much of anything is a bad thing. (Roman)
2. It is better to say nothing than not _____. (Roman)
3. _____ shovels of earth make a mountain. (Chinese)
4. Not having _____ is like not having anything. (Italian)
5. _____ many captains will sink the ship. (Danish)
6. It's never _____ late to ask what time it is. (Roman)

3 Look at the prompts and write sentences that are true for you.

1. I / rather / eat /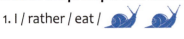

   _____

2. I / prefer / go / 👓 movie

   _____

3. I / like / travel / by / 🚆

   _____

4. I / prefer / have / pet 🐷

   _____

5. I / like / ride / 🚲 / to school

   _____

6. I / rather / have / 🍳 / for breakfast

   _____

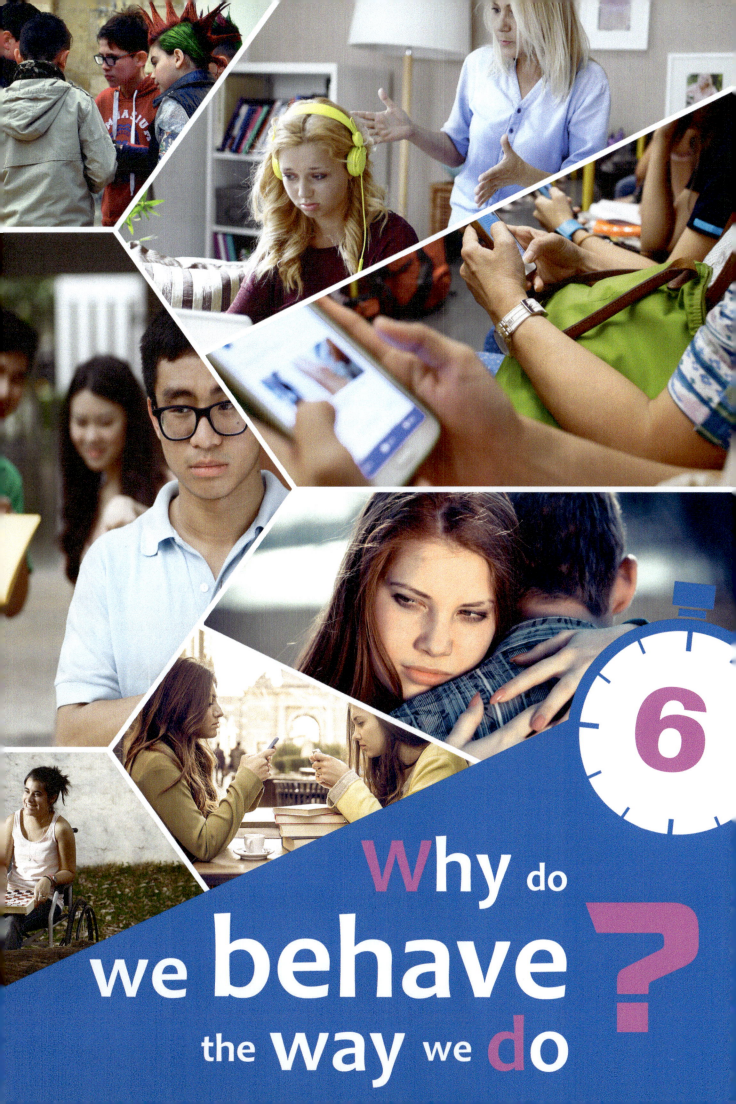

Vocabulary

1 Read the definitions of *dilemma*. Then look at the words below and cross out the ones that are not mentioned.

DILEMMA
noun | di·lem·ma

1: a situation in which you have to make a difficult choice

2: a situation in which a person has to choose between things that are all bad or unsatisfactory

3: a choice of actions that is based on moral reasons

4: a choice between two rights or two wrongs

concensus   actions
choice   agreement
alternative   moral
situation   difficult

2 Choose the best definition for you. Compare with a partner.

3 Read the dilemmas. Rank them from 1 (least difficult) to 6 (most difficult) in the boxes. Don't share your answers yet.

MORAL DILEMMAS

a A boy at Jim's school steals the phones of other kids. He then takes them to second-hand stores and sells them. He tells the storekeeper that he "finds" the phones in the street. Jim feels like he should **turn** the boy **in** to the police.

b Chris' best friend Lizzy is a graffiti artist. One day, the school bus is covered in graffiti. Then graffiti appears on the classroom walls. Chris knows that Lizzy is responsible, but he doesn't want to **tell on** his best friend. He knows Lizzy will **go on** writing graffiti all over the school.

c A group of Alexis' friends have started smoking. They are **underage** and she wants them to **give up** smoking. She **gets along with** all of them and she's worried that she might lose them as friends if she asks them to stop smoking.

d One day, Mark was in the school computer room and he opened an attachment which contained a computer virus. The virus has now infected every computer in the school. Nobody has **figured out** how the virus started, so Mark thinks he should **keep** it **to** himself.

e Tom and Lisa were going out for two months and they exchanged some personal photos. Now they have **broken up** and Tom is sharing the photos of Lisa online. Lisa has just **gotten over** the end of their relationship and she doesn't know this is happening. Lisa's friend Tara sees the photos.

f Gemma accidentally broke a window at school. Nobody saw her do it. Now her teacher will punish the whole class with a Saturday **detention** unless someone admits to breaking the window. Gemma has a lot of problems at school and she doesn't want to **own up to** it.

Stop and Think! How do values affect the way we solve dilemmas?

4 **Match the phrasal verbs in Activity 3 to their definitions.**

1. turn in
2. give up
3. get along with
4. break up
5. get over
6. tell on
7. go on
8. figure out
9. keep to (myself, yourself, etc.)
10. own up

____ a. solve a problem or find an answer
____ b. report someone to a parent or teacher for breaking a rule
____ c. end a relationship
____ d. confess you did a crime or broke a rule
____ e. not share some information with other people
____ f. report a criminal to the police
____ g. recover from a bad experience
____ h. continue doing something
____ i. stop doing something
____ j. be friends with

5 **Now, in small groups, identify the dilemma you each ranked number 6. Discuss why it was the most difficult one for you.**

> **Guess What!**
> If you are facing a very difficult decision or you have two very unpleasant alternatives to choose from you say, "I'm between a rock and a hard place."

6 🎧²⁸ **Circle the correct options to complete the sentences. Listen and check.**

1. Hannah's having problems in her French class because she doesn't **get** / **make** along with her teacher.
2. I cannot figure **off** / **out** what's wrong with my science homework.
3. I know I didn't go to basketball practice, but please don't **say** / **tell** on me.
4. I told Paula my secret and thankfully she **kept** / **took** it to herself.
5. Keep practicing the song–don't give **on** / **up**. You'll get it right soon.
6. I had to **own** / **tell** up to stealing the pen. I felt bad about it.
7. That movie was amazing! I can't believe the murderer's mother **gave** / **turned** him in to the police.
8. Simon never got **away** / **over** his parents' divorce.
9. Thalia isn't happy because she just broke **down** / **up** with her boyfriend.
10. The teacher told the class to stop laughing at the new boy, but they went **on** / **out** doing it.

7 **In pairs, take turns asking each other the questions.**

1. Who do you get along with best in your family?

   I get along with my older sister. She's my best friend.

2. When was the last time you gave up an activity because it was too difficult?
3. What difficult situations have you gotten over (e.g., telling on a friend)?
4. If someone tells you a secret, can you keep it to yourself or do you tell other people?
5. Have you ever owned up when you've done something wrong?

Glossary

underage: too young under the law to do something

detention: a punishment where students have to stay in a classroom or at school after their classes end

Grammar

1 Look at the pictures and number them in the order they happened.

2 🎧29 Listen to a radio show and check your answers to Activity 1.

3 🎧29 Listen again and complete the sentences.
1. She can't go to the _____ because she is too young.
2. _____ could use her sister's ID card to go to the disco. The sisters look similar.
3. Sienna might think Ashley took the wrong card by _____.
4. Ashley is _____ because the bouncer might look at her card.
5. She might not have any _____.
6. The bouncer could call her _____ or the police!
7. Ashley _____. They might send her to prison!

4 Look at the sentences in Activity 3 and answer the questions.
1. Which sentences refer to events that are possible?
2. Which sentences refer to events that are unlikely to happen?
3. Which sentences refer to events that are not possible?

might / could / may for possibility

Degrees of possibility

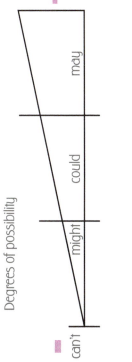

- can't = not possible
- might
- could + (not) verb in the base form
- may

5 Read each prompt and color the degree of possibility in each chart. Then write sentences with might, could and may.

1. Ashely / go to an underage disco
2. Ashley's parents / be mad at her
3. The police / **fine** Ashley's parents
4. Ashley / be grounded
5. Ashley / be happy with herself

6 In small groups, discuss the questions at the end of the radio show.
1. How bad was Ashley's crime?
2. Would you do the same in her situation?
3. What may happen next?

7 Think Fast! How many times have you been grounded? Why?

8 In your notebook, complete the sentences with might, could or may. Then compare with a partner.
1. If I invite my friends over when my parents are not home, …
2. If I don't get along with my best friend's friend, …
3. If my best friend breaks up with his / her boyfriend / girlfriend, …
4. If my friend doesn't keep my secret to herself / himself, …
5. If my best friend doesn't come to school on Monday, …

Guess What!
The most common punishment for teenagers in the US is being grounded. When you're grounded, you're not allowed to go out with your friends and you have to stay home. "You're grounded, young lady!"

Stop and Think! What is the legal age to consume alcoholic beverages in your country? Do you agree? Why or why not?

Glossary
bouncer: a person who provides security in a disco
fine: to require someone to pay money as a punishment

87

Reading & Writing

1 Work in groups of three. Each student reads one moral dilemma: A, B or C. Complete the table with information for your corresponding dilemma.

Dilemma ☐	What the problem is	My solution

Moral Dilemma A

Your school has a competition to write the best short story. The prize is to meet a famous author. Your friend Amber wins the competition and she is delighted. One day you are in Amber's house and you are looking at her books. You discover an identical story to the one she wrote. Amber **plagiarized** her winning story! If you tell on her, she can't meet the famous author—her hero. What do you do?

Moral Dilemma B

There is a new kid at your school and everyone is laughing at him. There is even a website about him which some bullies at the school designed. Nobody is sure who it was, but you know who it is because you saw some classmates working on it at school. You can tell a responsible adult. The only problem is that later the bullies might attack you. Perhaps it's best to keep it to yourself. What do you do?

Moral Dilemma C

You're in a small neighborhood shop. The staff knows your name and you get along with everyone there. You go there every week. One day, you go to buy some groceries for your parents. The cost is $4.50. You give the shopkeeper a $10 bill. In your **change**, he gives you a $50 bill instead of a $5 by mistake! He doesn't notice the error. What do you do?

Guess What!
In most countries, the bills that people use for paper money get bigger as the value increases. In the US, all dollar bills are the same size. A $100 bill is the same size as a $1 bill!

2 In your groups, follow the instructions.
  1. Take turns describing the moral dilemma you read and explain your solution to the other two students in your group.
  2. Discuss other possible solutions to each dilemma.
  3. Discuss which is the most difficult dilemma and why.

3 Read three possible solutions to moral dilemmas A, B and C. Write the correct number of each solution in Activity 1.

  1. I would point out the mistake and return the money. In spite of the fact that it wasn't my mistake, I would feel guilty if I kept it to myself. Also, an employee may lose his / her job because money has disappeared from the shop. I get along well with them, so I don't want anything bad to happen.

  2. Even though she broke the rules, I wouldn't tell anyone in this case. It isn't my responsibility to tell on her. I could lose a friend, and friends are more important than competitions.

  3. Despite the risk, I would tell the bullies to delete the website. The most important thing is to stop the bullying, or it could go on and on. Although the bullies would escape with no punishment, this might stop the problem.

Glossary
plagiarize: to steal or copy the writing of another person and to say it is your own work

change: the money you get back after you buy something

4 Underline the phrases to express contrast in Activity 3.

5 Complete the sentences with words and phrases to express contrast. More than one answer is possible.

1. _____ I'm very shy, I was nice to the new girl when she joined our class.
2. Our neighbors had a loud party all night and the music went on and on. I was able to do my homework _____ the noise.
3. The boys covered the train in graffiti, _____ it is a crime.
4. Nick made a joke about his girlfriend to his friends and she heard it. _____ the joke, they didn't break up.
5. Noel was grounded by his parents, but he didn't say sorry _____ the punishment.

6 Choose one of the dilemmas below. Then complete the table. In your notebook, write a paragraph with your solution.

Be Strategic!
When writing, use specific words and phrases to express contrast.

Use *although* and *even though* in front of a subject and verb to join two sentences.
Although I was late, the teacher wasn't angry.
Even though I told her the truth, she didn't believe me.

Use *despite* and *in spite of* with a noun.
Despite the bad weather, we ate outside.
I owned up in spite of the consequences.

Add *despite the fact that* and *in spite of the fact that* with a subject + verb.
Despite the fact that I hated the food, I ate it all.
We got a taxi in spite of the fact that it was expensive.

Moral Dilemma D
Cindy is the best singer in her after-school music group. Everybody loves to hear her sing. Then one day, a TV company invites the group to come on their TV show. The director of the music group announces that another girl, Helen, will be the lead singer on TV. The director is Helen's mom.

Moral Dilemma E
You and your friends are playing soccer next to a factory. One of your friends accidentally kicks the ball over the fence into the factory. There is a danger sign on the fence. There is a hole and you can get through it. Your friends all tell you to get the ball and they will laugh at you if you don't do it.

The problem	
How you feel about about the problem	
Sentence with contrast word or phrase	
Your solution	

Culture

1  Circle the correct options to complete the fact file. Then listen and check.

South Korea

Fact File

The Korean peninsula is in East (1) **Africa / Asia**. The peninsula is divided into two countries: democratic South Korea and communist (2) **North / West** Korea. South Korea is one of the world's most technologically advanced countries. It is home to many famous technology companies like LG and (3) **Samsung / Sony**. The capital, (4) **Pyongyang / Seoul**, was the host of the Olympic Games in 1988 and the soccer World Cup in 2002 along with Japan. This was the first World Cup to be hosted by two countries. The most famous person from South Korea is the pop star Psy, and you might know his song "Gangnam Style," which was a massive hit in (5) **2012 / 2015**.

2 Read Madison's blog. Then match the number of tips to the pictures.

Blog | Home | Smart Travel

A hard homecoming in Korea

Saturday, May 7 / by Madison Khim

Hi, I'm Madison Khim. My parents moved to the US from South Korea and I was born in Los Angeles. Last summer, I went "home" to Korea for the first time ever and boy, did I break the rules! You might do the same if you go there, so here's my advice to stop you from making the same mistakes as me! These are my tips.

Tip 1
The first thing is to take your shoes off in the home. Even though I knew that, when I visited a school on my trip, I went on wearing my shoes. Korean students have special slippers for the classroom!

Tip 2
I also made a mistake with my Korean grandmother. I wrote her name in red ink–you never do that in Korea! You might offend people because you only write dead people's names in red ink. Luckily, I get along well with Grandma, so I apologized.

Tip 3
Oh, and I upset my cousins, too. I asked them to come over to me with one finger. Koreans don't do that! In the end, I figured out that they ask you to come closer with their hand down and their fingers pointing down. It's very similar to our "go away" sign!

Tip 4
Meal times were difficult, too. The food is very spicy so you may want to blow your nose at the table, but you can't because that's very rude. You have to get up and do it in the bathroom where people can't see you.

Tip 5
I made my last mistake on my last morning. I got on the bus to go to the airport and the bus driver asked me to move. Why? In Korea, the front seats of the bus are only for senior citizens. Young people sit at the back.

Lots of people make these mistakes and usually you couldn't offend people, but because I'm Korean-American, everyone expected me to know the rules. But now you know, when in Korea, do as the Koreans do!

Posted by Madison Khim at 8:25   1 Comment
Labels: Korean Etiquette

90

Community X

Stop and Think! Why is it useful to know the customs of a place you have never been to?

3 Read the blog again. Circle *T* (True) or *F* (False).

1. Madison lived in South Korea when she was a baby.   T   F
2. Koreans don't wear any shoes in school.   T   F
3. The ink color is important in Korea.   T   F
4. Koreans ask you to come to them with one finger.   T   F
5. Korean food is very hot.   T   F
6. Madison sat at the back of the bus by mistake.   T   F

4 **Think Fast!** Name five tips you would give a friend that will visit your country for the first time. (5 min)

5 Complete the comment to Madison's blog with the words in the box.

eyes   age   cultures   socks   mistakes   royalty

Blog   Comment   Smart Travels   X

lemonboots Sunday, May 8

Hi Madison,

I went to Korea a couple of months ago and our (1) _____ are so different! I made new friends and they immediately asked me my (2) _____! Apparently, it's normal to do it just after meeting a Korean. Another thing I found fascinating is the **bowing**. Koreans do it for meeting and greeting. Although a full, right-angled bow is just for meeting (3) _____, a short bow with (4) _____ closed is perfectly normal. Despite all the (5) _____ a **foreigner** could make, Koreans are very patient. Yes, Koreans take their shoes off to go inside a house, so pack clean and hole-free (6) _____!

My two cents,
Alison

Reply

Glossary
bowing:
foreigner: a person who is from a country that is not your own

Project

1 In pairs, read the comments. Discuss the ones that you agree with.

1. Parents today have no time for their children. They're always working. ☐
2. Smart phones are terrible. I feel anxious whenever I get a message or a tweet. ☐
3. There's too much violence on TV. ☐
4. It's a man's world. We need equal rights for men and women. ☐
5. You can't hang out outside anymore because it's too dangerous. ☐
6. Parents do not have the right to monitor their teenager's activities online. ☐
7. Teenagers should not wear a school uniform. ☐
8. Nobody cares about bullying at school. ☐
9. People in my neighborhood care about the environment. ☐

Stop and Think! What are the biggest worries that teenagers have today in your country: at school, at home, in society?

2 🎧31 Read the responses below. Write the correct letter to each comment in Activity 1. Then listen and check.

a. **I don't think that's true** because if you tell any teacher, they will stop it.

b. **I disagree.** Where I live we do it all the time and we've never had an incident.

c. **I agree up to a point, but** things are better for women today than in the past.

d. **I see your point, but** it is more expensive for parents to spend so much money on clothes.

e. **I think that's right.** Everyone separates waste, for example.

f. **That's absolutely right.** That's why many people's grandparents look after the kids.

g. **I totally disagree.** Mine is essential. I need to be connected to the Internet all the time.

h. **I partly agree, but** sometimes they need to protect their children.

i. **I agree.** There's blood everywhere. It's horrible.

3 Write the phrases in bold in Activity 2 in the correct columns.

Phrases to Agree	Phrases to Disagree	Phrases to Partly Agree

When using social media we're giving up our privacy.

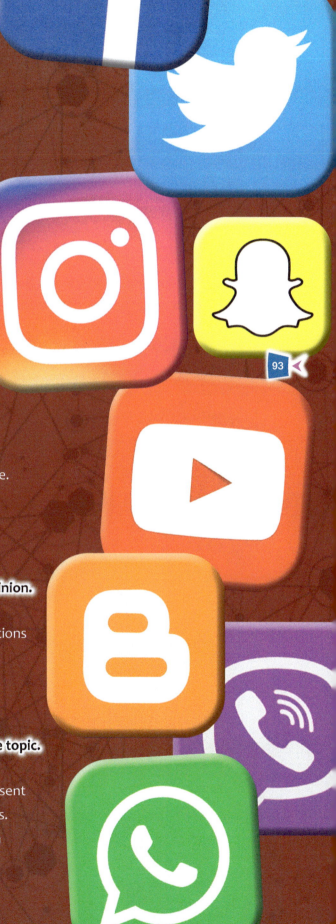

4 You will have a class debate. In your notebook, follow the steps to get ready.
1. Make a list of all the social media websites / apps you know.
2. What do you use each one for and how often?
3. Think about your privacy. Can you control what another person posts or shares about you on social media?
4. Make a list of three bad experiences people could have related to social media.
5. Decide if you agree or disagree with the statement above.

5 Think Fast! Name the three most popular social media in your country. *(1 min)*

6 Work in small groups with classmates who share your opinion. In your notebook, follow the steps.
1. Provide a context for your argument. Answer the questions who, where, when and why.
2. Write three reasons that support your argument.
3. Think of a conclusion.

7 Work with a group that doesn't share your opinion on the topic. Follow the steps to have a debate.
1. Those who agree with the statement of the debate present their argument. Then those who disagree present theirs.
2. Use the phrases to agree, disagree or partly agree from Activity 3.
3. Present your conclusions.

Review

1 Match the captions to the pictures.

1. He had no choice but to turn himself in.
2. We let her go on drawing everywhere.
3. Can you figure out what they wanted to represent?
4. They don't get along.

2 Match the sentence halves.

1. Nobody owned…
2. My brother failed English. I will keep…
3. Dan's dog died and he hasn't gotten…
4. I don't like my violin lessons. I want to give…

a. them up.
b. over it.
c. it to myself.
d. up to eating all the cookies.

3 Complete the dialogues with the phrasal verbs in the box.

```
break up   figure out   get over   get along with   give up   go on
keep it to   own up   tell on   turn him in
```

1. **BETH:** Do you need some help with your math homework?
   DON: Yes, please! Look at problem 6. I can't _____ the answer at all.

2. **SUSAN:** Mom and Dad know one of us came back home late last night. You should _____ and tell them it was you.
   CURTIS: But I came in as silently as I could!

3. **SALLY:** Joanna wants to _____ with her boyfriend.
   ANNA: Why? I thought they were happy together.

4. **VICKY:** Are you friends with Nick?
   TOM: No, I don't _____ him at all.

5. **NINA:** I saw you steal that paper from the school printer. I'm going to _____ you.
   HARRIET: No, please don't. I'll return it.

6. **LUCY:** I'm too tired. I can't run any more.
   BROOKLYN: Don't _____! We can do it!

7. **MARIE:** Shawn didn't get the part he wanted in the school play. He's really disappointed.
   ERIC: He'll _____ it. He'll feel better soon.

8. **LUKE:** You know my secret now, so _____ yourself.
   ROBBIE: I won't tell anyone. You have my word.

9. **PETE:** What happened at the end of the movie?
   ALEXIS: The thief's wife decided to _____ to the police.

10. **WALT:** Paul saw a shark when he was surfing!
    KAY: Yes, but he says in despite of it, he's going to _____ surfing.

◀ **Unscramble the sentences.**

1. could / a / tomorrow / quiz / we / surprise / have
   _____

2. my / year / leave / next / home / may / brother
   _____

3. your / win / soccer / the / league / team / might
   _____

4. a / center / we / to / bus / the / city / can't / get
   _____

5. skipped / because / be / class / may / Sam / he / history / grounded
   _____

◢ **In pairs, look at the extreme close-ups and discuss what they are. Use** *might, could* **or** *may*.

(This extreme close-up might be…)   (I don't think so. It could be…)

Just for Fun

1 Circle ten phrasal verbs in the word snake.

getoverturninggiveuptellonbreakupgoonfigureoutkeeptoyourselfownupgetalongwith

2 Explain what might, could or may happen in the situations.
1. Your 📱 makes a sound.
2. You get home and you see a 💡 in one of the windows.
3. You hear a noise in the middle of the night and you walk down the 🪜.
4. Your 👨‍🏫 wants to see you after class.
5. There is nobody in your classroom, except 👊.
6. A 📦 arrives in the mail for you.

3 Complete the sentences with the celebrities' names.

Adele

James Corden

Julia Roberts

Tom Hiddlestone

1. _____ walked barefoot on the red carpet in the 2016 Cannes Film Festival. She did it as a protest against the festival organizers who didn't allow women in their fifties to wear flats.

2. _____ is a UNICEF Ambassador because he wants to help children who suffer in humanitarian emergencies like war. For him, education is a way to help them get over the horrors of war and be safe.

3. _____ has a segment in his show called Carpool Karaoke. Despite the fact that he is driving, he manages to make the celebrities sing their most iconic songs. He gets along well with them and they have very funny moments.

4. _____ forgot the lyrics at a live concert in England. She owned up immediately and apologized laughing. Her fans love her more than ever despite her mistake.

Vocabulary

1 Think Fast! In your notebook, write four types of: meat, fish, fruit and vegetables.
3 min

a

2 Read the descriptions of what Mr. Stickman is doing (1–6). Then write the correct number of description in each picture (a–f).

1. He is **baking** a pie.
2. He is **grilling** hamburgers.
3. He is **frying** some eggs.
4. He is **boiling** some rice.
5. He is **roasting** a turkey.
6. He is **steaming** some vegetables.

d

3 🎧32 Label the dishes below with the words in the box that indicate how they are cooked. Then listen and check.

> baked   boiled   fried   grilled   (raw) not cooked   steamed   roasted

dumplings

1 Dim sum

2 British Sunday lunch

3 Goulash

4 Acarajé

pastry

5 Baklava

6 Ceviche

7 Tandoori chicken

4 🎧³² **Listen again and complete the sentences with the words in the box.**

> sour   chewy   raw   bland   sticky   crispy   spicy

1. The stereotype of British cooking is that it's _____ and doesn't taste like anything.
2. There are usually big pieces of meat in goulash, so it's _____.
3. Acarajé are lovely and a little _____ on the outside.
4. At the end, you pour more honey on it, so baklava is very sweet and _____, too.
5. Ceviche is made with _____ fish, so it's served cold.
6. Ceviche is also covered in juice from lemons and limes, which taste _____.
7. The chicken is covered in red chili powder, so it is very _____.

5 **Write a dish or ingredient that you can describe with the following words. Compare with a partner.**

1. bland _____
2. chewy _____
3. crispy _____
4. raw _____
5. sour _____
6. spicy _____
7. sticky _____

Stop and Think! What dish from your country is identified around the world? What does it taste like?

6 **In pairs, take turns answering the questions about Activity 3.**

1. Have you ever tried any of the dishes?
2. Which one would you like to try? Why?
3. Which one wouldn't you like to try? Why not?
4. Are there any dishes from your country that are similar to any of these dishes?

Glossary

dumplings: a piece of food that is wrapped in dough and cooked
pastry: dough that is used to make pies and other baked goods

Grammar

1 **Discuss these questions with a partner.**
1. Where did you celebrate the last New Year?
2. Who were you with?
3. What did you eat?
4. Who cooked the food?
5. Did you have fun?

2 🎧³³ **Listen to Erin talk about her last New Year. Write her answers to the questions in Activity 1.**

3 🎧³⁴ **Listen and cross (X) T (True) or F (False). Correct the false information.**

1. My sister and I were invited to the party.   T F
2. **Polka dots** are worn by everyone. The dots are circles. Circles are thought to bring prosperity because they look like **coins**.   T F
3. At New Year in the Philippines, all the adults jump high in the air when the clock strikes 12. It's believed that if you jump high, you'll grow tall!   T F
4. I was given some amazing **noodles**. They were cooked by Lisa's grandpa. He is 82!   T F
5. Noodles are eaten by Filipinos at New Year. The noodles are long, so they are said to represent long hair!   T F
6. Chicken and fish are not eaten at **New Year's Eve**. It's bad luck on that day—they are thought to represent **scarcity** of food.   T F
7. The house isn't cleaned on New Year's Eve. It is thought you would **sweep** the good luck out of your house!   T F

Glossary

noodles:

polka dots:

coins: metal money
New Year's Eve: December 31st
scarcity: very little or not enough of something
sweep: clean a floor with a broom

The Passive

Present	Active	Everyone wears polka dots. Subject — Verb in present — Object
	Passive	Polka dots are worn by everyone. Subject — be + past participle — by + doer
Past	Active	Lisa's grandpa cooked the noodles. Subject — Verb in past — Object
	Passive	The noodles were cooked by Lisa's grandpa. Subject — be + past participle — by + doer

Uses of the Passive
1. The action is more important than doer of the action.
2. The doer of the action is unknown.
3. The doer is not important.

4 Focus on the uses of the passive. Write A (Action), U (Unknown) or NI (not important).

1. In Mexico, when the clock strikes twelve, suitcases are taken out of the house to bring travel the coming year. ☐
2. My brother and I were invited to the party. ☐
3. In the Philippines, the house isn't cleaned on New Year's Eve. ☐
4. I was given some amazing noodles. ☐
5. My cousins were taken to the movies on New Year's Day last year. ☐
6. In the Philippines, chicken and fish aren't eaten at New Year. ☐

5 Change these sentences into the passive.

1. In Denmark, people often break plates to celebrate New Year.
   _____
2. People often wear red at New Year in my country.
   _____
3. In Spain, people eat twelve grapes at midnight at New Year.
   _____
4. In Scotland, people sing the traditional song "Auld Lang Syne" at New Year.
   _____
5. My family held the New Year's party last year.
   _____
6. In Greece, people put a coin in a New Year's cake for good luck.
   _____

6 In your notebook, compare New Year in your country with New Year in the Philippines. Write sentences using the passive. Look at the example to help you.

> I'm from China, so New Year is celebrated in February. It isn't celebrated on January 1st. Lots of parties are held with fireworks. Sweet dumplings are served and red envelopes are given to kids with lucky money.

Listening & Writing

1 Read the introduction to an interview and discuss the questions.

1. What are the advantages of living in a place like Easter Island?
2. What are the disadvantages?

What's it like in your country?
Diego is 13 and he lives on Easter Island or Rapa Nui (the Polynesian name). The island is part of Chile and it is located in the Pacific Ocean. It was formed by volcanic eruptions. Easter Island is one of the most remote places on Earth. It is 2,075 kilometers away from the next nearest island. Only about 6,000 people live there.

2 🎧35 Listen to Diego talk about his life on Easter Island. Number the pictures in the order they are mentioned.

3 🎧35 Complete the sentences. Then listen again to check.

1. Everyone knows our famous giant _____ heads.
2. The Tapati Festival is held in _____ and _____ each year.
3. To cook the dish umu, you make a hole in the ground. Then, meat or _____ is put in the ground.
4. I love astronomy – **stargazing**. I was given a telescope for my by birthday by my _____.
5. On Easter Island, there isn't a lot of _____.

Guess What!
In 2012, archaeologists excavated a couple of giant heads and discovered they actually have bodies! They are standing figures with torsos up to the waist that were buried by dirt over the centuries.

4 🎧³⁵ Work in groups of four. Each student listens for more information about their corresponding topic. In your notebook, take notes.
1. Student A, the stone heads.
2. Student B, the Tapati Festival.
3. Student C, the dish umu.
4. Student D, stargazing on Easter Island.

5 In the same groups, discuss the questions.
1. Were you able to identify the details of your part of the information?
2. Was it easy or difficult? Why?
3. Was it necessary to listen to the recording more than once?
4. Were you able to identify details about the other topics?

6 Read six common mistakes in writing.
1. Not using a capital letter for a language (Spanish).
2. Not using a capital letter for a nationality (Canadian).
3. Forgetting an apostrophe in a possessive (John's, the team's).
4. Forgetting an apostrophe in a contraction (I'm).
5. Using an ellipsis (…) in the wrong place.
6. Using too many exclamation marks (!).

Be Strategic!
When you you listen to a recording several times, listen for more detailed information each time.

After you have understood the general idea of a recording, listen for supporting information.

Supporting information is extra information about the ideas in the recording.

Don't try to listen for everything at the same time. Choose one topic, and listen carefully for the supporting information.

Stop and Think! What is the difference between exclamation marks (!), ellipsis (…) and a period (.)? Which one do we use most in writing?

7 Read the text and find the mistakes described in Activity 6. Then correct them.

First impressions of Easter Island – Marcela Costa

I just arrived on Easter Island for the very first time! It was a five-hour flight from Chile! That was a long time in the air! I expected a hot tropical island, but actually it's raining today! It's May and everyone tells me that it is the rainiest month of the year!

The island is beautiful and people are very friendly… Everybody smiles all the time. That's just great. There is one problem and that is that there are lots of tourists. Everywhere I go, I see people with their cameras. I hear lots of different languages too, like English, Spanish and french. Interestingly, my parents and I aren't the only brazilian tourists here. There are some surfers from Rio here too. In fact, Easter Island is a surfers paradise. Its because there are big waves here! Maybe I'll try it myself while I'm here …

Glossary
stargazing: the practice of looking at the stars

NEW ZEALAND

1 🎧 36 Listen and complete the fact file on New Zealand.

New Zealand is in the (1) _____ Hemisphere. On maps, it is often placed near Australia, but actually, they are 4,155 kilometers apart. That's almost the distance between (2) _____ and Iraq. There are two main islands in New Zealand: North Island and South Island. Most people live in North Island, where the (3) _____, Wellington, is, as well as the largest city, Auckland. About (4) _____ million people live in New Zealand.
(5) _____ percent of them are Māori–the original inhabitants of the islands before the Europeans arrived. Its name comes from Zeeland, which is a region in (6) _____.

• Auckland
• Wellington

2 Answer the quiz. Then match the questions with the pictures.

What do you know about New Zealand?

1. In 1893, New Zealand became the first country in the world to give the vote in elections to all…
   a. adult men.
   b. adult women.
   c. sixteen year olds.

2. New Zealand has the world's… street.
   a. most illuminated
   b. longest
   c. **steepest**

3. New Zealand is home to the world's largest…
   a. cricket.
   b. ant.
   c. snake.

4. Which kiwi didn't originally come from New Zealand?
   a. People called Kiwis
   b. The kiwi bird
   c. The kiwi fruit

5. Which movies were filmed in New Zealand?
   a. The Hobbit
   b. The Hunger Games
   c. The Lord of the Rings

6. What is New Zealand's national sport?
   a. Baseball
   b. Rugby
   c. Cricket

Hāngi
A Traditional Māori Meal

A hāngi is a traditional Māori style of cooking in New Zealand. The food is steamed in an oven in the ground. This style of cooking is used all around the Pacific—in Chile it's called *Curanto* and in Easter Island it's called *Umu*. First, dig a hole in the ground. It is commonly believed that the hole should be very deep, but that's not true. The hole should be big enough to fit the basket with food. The secret of a good hāngi is to have good rocks and good wood. The rocks need to be volcanic to absorb the heat better. Light the fire 3 to 5 hours before you want to start cooking. The hāngi consists of beef, chicken or pork. It also has vegetables like potatoes, pumpkins or carrots. **Season** the food as you wish and cover the hāngi with banana leaves or **tinfoil**. Cover it with dirt so the hāngi is steamed. Uncover it after 3 hours and dig in!

Glossary

steep: rising or falling very sharply
light: to cause (something) to burn
season: to add salt, pepper, spices, etc.
tinfoil: a thin sheet of shiny metal that is used especially for cooking

- [ ] Light the fire beforehand.
- [ ] Cover the hāngi to steam it.
- [ ] Dig a hole in the ground.
- [ ] Uncover the hāngi and serve.
- [ ] Season the food.
- [ ] Find volcanic rocks and wood.

105

6 Read the text and number the steps below.

3 🎧 37 Listen to check your answers.

4 🎧 37 Work in groups of three. Listen again for supporting information.

1. Student A, make notes about questions 1 and 4.
2. Student B, make notes about questions 2 and 5.
3. Student C, make notes about questions 3 and 6.

My Question Numbers		
Supporting Information		

5 Compare your answers to Activity 4 with another group. Then listen again if necessary.

Guess What!
In New Zealand, only 5% of the population are humans, the rest are animals.

Project

In England, bacon, fried eggs, sausages, tomatoes, mushrooms, toast and baked beans are eaten for breakfast. Tea is drunk instead of coffee.

In the US, pancakes with butter and maple syrup are eaten for breakfast.

In France, freshly baked croissants are eaten for breakfast. Oh, la la!

In Iceland, hot oatmeal sprinkled with raisins or nuts and brown sugar is eaten for breakfast. It is eaten to warm up on a cold morning!

1 Look at some breakfasts from around the world. Discuss the questions with a partner.

1. Which one would you like to try? Why?
2. Which one wouldn't you like to try? Why?
3. What do you usually have for breakfast?
4. Does your family ever have something special for breakfast? What is it? When do you eat it?

 2 **Think Fast!** Name the ingredients of your favorite breakfast.

Guess What! The English word "dinner" comes from the French word "disnar," which means "breakfast."

3 Write the correct number of each item.

- [ ] a bag of flour
- [ ] butter
- [ ] an egg
- [ ] a frying pan
- [ ] a teaspoon of baking powder
- [ ] maple syrup
- [ ] some milk
- [ ] salt
- [ ] some sugar
- [ ] a whisk

4 In pairs, discuss how to make pancakes with the ingredients in Activity 3.

5 🎧³⁸ Complete the pancake recipe with the missing sentences. Then listen and check.

a. Serve it with some butter and maple syrup.
b. **Whisk** all the ingredients together. This makes **batter**.
c. In another **bowl**, mix 125 milliliters of milk with the egg.
d. When it's hot, add some of the batter.

---

1. In one bowl, mix 125 grams of flour with the baking powder.
2. Add some salt and sugar to the powder.
3. ☐
4. Melt some butter and add it to the milk and egg.
5. Combine the milk and egg with the flour and baking powder.
6. ☐
7. Melt some more butter in a frying pan.
8. ☐
9. Once one side is cooked, turn it over in the pan.
10. ☐

Note: You can make your pancakes more delicious by adding different ingredients such as raisins, cranberries, nuts, bananas, chocolate chips, etc.

6 In small groups, think of a popular dish from your country. Write a recipe for how to make it. Follow the steps.
- Choose a dish that doesn't have a lot of ingredients (about six is a good number).
- Don't choose a dish that is very difficult to cook. Choose one that you can fry, boil, bake, roast, grill or steam.
- Check the recipe with ideas online. Look up the ingredients in English.
- Write the recipe like the one in Activity 5.
- Exchange your recipe with another group's. Ask them if the ingredients and steps in your recipe are clear.
- Decide if the other group's recipe is clear and if you could follow the steps. If not, give them feedback.

Glossary

baking powder: a white powder that is used to make baked foods light and fluffy

whisk: to stir or beat (eggs, sauces, etc.) with a whisk or fork

batter: a mixture of different ingredients that is cooked and eaten

bowl:

 **Stop and Think!** They say "if you can read, you can cook." Do you agree? Why or why not?

Review

1 Unscramble the words to complete the e-mail.

Cancel	Cooking disaster!	Send

To: Grandma
From: Tom

Hi Grandma,
As you know, Mom always cooks in our house and she's the best. She even (1) _____ (sabek) her own bread. Yesterday, she was sick, so Dad and I cooked dinner. It was a disaster!
We made a *chilli con carne*. In the recipe, you (2) _____ (osrat) the meat first, but we forgot to turn the oven on. The beef was (3) _____ (war) when we started cooking!
Then we (4) _____ (defir) some onion and garlic. That was OK, but the oil went everywhere. On our clothes, on the stove, everywhere! Oops!
Dad boiled the rice while I cooked the rest of the food. Unfortunately, a soccer game was on TV, so he forgot the rice. The water (5) _____ (odebli) over the pan and made more mess.
When we finished the *chilli con carne*, we knew something was wrong. It smelled disgusting! We couldn't eat it, so Dad drove to a local restaurant and bought some (6) _____ (lilgerd) chicken and (7) _____ (edetmas) vegetables. When we served it to Mom, she was like "Mmm, this is delicious and so healthy! You guys should cook every day!"
Will you show me how to cook *chilli con carne*, please?
Tom

2 Cross out the wrong word in each sentence.

1. We need some hot water to **boil** / **grill** / **steam** these vegetables.
2. We usually eat these tomatoes **fried** / **boiled** / **raw** by putting olive oil on them.
3. To cook this dish, you need to **bake** / **boil** / **roast** it in the oven.
4. The chicken is a bit black because we **fried** / **grilled** / **steamed** it a little too long.
5. **Fried** / **Raw** / **Steamed** carrots are good for you because they don't contain any fat.

3 Label the pictures with the words in the box.

sour   spicy   chewy   raw   bland   crispy   sticky

4 Write the correct number of response to each question.

1. Mom, my chicken is still 🟥 in the middle. It's a bit raw.
2. I can't see out the 🪟. Are you steaming something?
3. We roasted the 🐔 for too long.
4. Shall we get 🍬 or savory snacks?
5. Oh dear. This 🍲 is really bland.
6. Your lemon 🥧 tastes too sour.
7. So tacos are from 🇲🇽 and you fill them with fried beef.

a. Candy and chocolate–Grandpa and Grandma have a sweet tooth.
b. That's right. Any meat, really. We also put a spicy sauce on them.
c. Yes, it's broccoli. It's the best way to cook it so it stays crispy.
d. Don't eat it! I'll grill it again for another five minutes.
e. It needs more sugar. It's my mistake. It was the first time I baked one.
f. It doesn't taste like anything, does it? Maybe I forgot to add the salt!
g. I know. It's burnt, isn't it?

5 Write the correct number of sentence in each picture. Then change the sentences into the passive.

Traditions Around the World

1. Brazilians celebrate Carnival in Rio de Janeiro every year.
_____
_____

2. People in the US and Canada celebrate Thanksgiving in November.
_____
_____

3. Mexicans made a beautiful offering on last year's Day of the Dead.
_____
_____

4. Russians culminate the White Nights Festival with the Scarlet Sails celebration.
_____
_____

5. Last year, the running bulls in Pamplona injured hundreds of people.
_____
_____

Just for Fun

The World's Weirdest Dishes

1 Write the number that describes each dish.

①

Steamed Steak
One of the most popular dishes in Scotland is steamed steak. Scotland has lots of rain and lots of grass. The grass is eaten by cows and so a lot of beef is produced in the country. They have so much water from the rain, that steaming is a popular way of cooking. Steamed steak is a Scottish classic.

②

Thousand-year-old Eggs
This is an old, old recipe from China. An egg is preserved for several months. Of course that means it becomes rotten, it goes bad. The egg white changes color from white to brown and the yolk changes color from yellow to green. The taste is like a normal boiled egg.

③

Rotten Shark
Rotten shark is a popular dish in Iceland. Food goes rotten when it goes bad, but people in Iceland love this classic dish. A dead shark is buried under the ground for several months until it goes rotten. Then it is dug up and cured for two more months. At the end, white meat is produced—a local delicacy.

④

Deadly Fish
It is said that fish is good for your health. Japan's fugu may be the exception. This fish is popular in Japan and it is said to be delicious. Unfortunately, it is also poisonous if you eat the wrong part. Many people are killed every year by eating this fish!

2 Find ten food words and dishes in the word search.

```
B E E F Q J T X W Z
X C R O I S S A N T
D P A R B U T T E R
G I D B R O U G P T
O E P A N C A K E U
U R R A I D H S N R
L I B A K L A V A K
A C A R A J E E A E
S E Z R E A D Q A Y
H D U M P L I N G S
```

3 One dish in Activity 1 is false. Guess which one.

4 Look at the picture for forty seconds. Then close your books. Name all the food you can.

Podcast Vocabulary

1 Work in small groups and discuss the questions.
1. What are the most common jobs in your country or region?
2. What jobs does your country or region need? Why?
3. What jobs do people in your family have?

Stop and Think! How is talent related to the job that someone chooses to do?

2 Read the introduction to a podcast. Then label the pictures with the jobs in the box.

animation director   chef   sports coach
computer game programmer   crime scene investigator
graffiti artist   marine biologist   travel writer

We all want our dream job, but only some people are lucky enough to get it. We speak to eight lucky people who love what they do. Maybe one day, you could be one, too?

3 🎧39 Listen and number the pictures in Activity 2 in the order you hear them.

4 🎧39 Complete the sentences with the words in the box. Then listen again and check.

apply   contract   deal   make   long   manage   qualifications   retire

1. I'm a travel writer. I got this job because of my languages. I speak Spanish and English. I also have the right _____ – I have a degree in Journalism.
2. I'm a graffiti artist. It's an amazing job. I have a _____ to paint an advertising campaign. It's going to be so cool.
3. Unfortunately, I had to _____ after I broke my leg very badly. Now I'm an ice skating coach and I train kids in speed skating.
4. I always dreamed of becoming a chef. The only bad thing about my job is the _____ hours. We work evenings and weekends.
5. I studied character animation and today I'm an animation director. I _____ a team of artists and I tell them what to do.
6. So when I saw the job advertisement for a computer game programmer, I decided to _____ for it.
7. I'm a scientist, a marine biologist and I work with sharks. Working with animals is a dream. I really feel like I _____ a difference.
8. In fact, I'm a crime scene investigator. It's my dream job, but we see some terrible things and we _____ with many different problems.

5 Complete the table with jobs from Activity 2. Add more jobs.

Jobs				
-ant	-er	-or	-ist	Other
accountant	builder	doctor	dentist	musician
				nurse

6 Think Fast! Think of one more job…

1. that you can do outdoors.
2. that you can only do if you have qualifications like a university degree.
3. where you work with animals.
4. where you need a strong stomach.
5. where you can make a difference in people's lives.
6. where you can earn a lot of money.
7. where you have very long hours.

7 Look at the jobs on both pages and complete the table below. Then compare it with a partner.

This is my dream job	This job would be impossible for me	I know someone who would like this job	I would never do this job

1 Read the descriptions of each job. Then write the correct number of the description in each picture.

a

b

c

d

e

f

1. A paleontologist is a scientist who studies fossils. The biggest fossil ever, which was found in Argentina, is a two-meter leg bone from a dinosaur.
2. Formula 1 is a sport which features the world's fastest cars. Formula 1 drivers, who come from many different countries, risk their lives every time they are in a race.
3. A DJ is a person who plays music in nightclubs. The job title DJ, which means "disk jockey," was first used in the 1940s.
4. A travel writer is a person who writes guidebooks. Guidebooks like *Lonely Planet*, which comes from Australia, sell millions of books every year.
5. A pet groomer is a person who cuts the hair of animals. It is too difficult to cut the hair of certain animals at home, for example, dogs like a shih tzu, which have very long hair.
6. Many people teach activities like yoga that help people to relax. Yoga, which comes from India, is now popular all over the world.

▶ 114

2 Look again at the sentences in Activity 1 and follow the instructions.
   1. Circle three defining relative clauses.
   2. Underline three non-defining relative clauses.

3 Replace *that* in the defining relative clauses with *who* or *which*. Write the relative pronouns on the lines.
   1. A surgeon is a specialist doctor that performs operations. _____
   2. My dad is an Indian chef and he makes a curry that tastes amazing. _____
   3. Matt has a job as a graffiti artist that pays $200 a week. _____
   4. If you're looking for work, this is a website that has lots of job ads. _____
   5. The marine biologist that was on TV has the same name as me. _____
   6. She's the one that coaches our football team! _____

Defining and Non-defining Relative Clauses

A relative clause gives extra information about a noun.
- A defining relative clause tells you what a noun is.

A paleontologist is a scientist <u>who studies fossils</u>.

- A non-defining relative clause gives you more information about a noun. It is separated from the rest of the sentence with commas (,).

The biggest fossil ever, <u>which was found in Argentina</u>, is a two-meter leg bone from a dinosaur.

- We use relative pronouns
  who for people,
  which for animals and things and
  that for people, animals and things.

4 Rewrite the sentences to include the extra information. Write the extra information between commas.

1. Bikram is my favorite type of yoga. It is done in a sauna-like room.
   _____
2. My sister works as a paleontologist. She is 21.
   _____
3. Orthodontists are very well paid. They help straighten your teeth.
   _____
4. J.K. Rowling is the author of the Harry Potter books. She's British.
   _____
5. Mr. Clements teaches us drama. He will be the director of the school play.
   _____

Defining Relative Clauses

Sometimes the relative pronoun in a defining relative clause is the subject of the clause.
A paleontologist is a scientist who studies fossils.
Sometimes the relative pronoun in a defining relative clause is the object of the clause.
Ivan programmed a computer game which I play all the time.
If the relative pronoun is the object of the clause, we can cut it from the sentence.
Ivan programmed a computer game which I play all the time.
We cannot cut the relative pronoun from a non-defining relative clause.

5 Cross out six relative pronouns that can be omitted in the article.

What's it really like to be a travel writer?

People think travel writers live a life of luxury. However, most of the travel journalists who I know don't think it's a dream job. Travel writers spend months in hotel rooms which they hate. These hotels can be small or dirty, or miles from the center of town. Writers have to visit all the places which they are going to describe. With only a year to write each book, travel writers also have very little time. They often need the help of local people who can give them advice about the local area. The people who I often ask for tips are the hotel staff, like receptionists and waiters. They often know all the places that tourists never find.
I have worked as a travel writer for 10 years and I still love it, but it is not a job for everyone. One day you could be in a five-star hotel. The next day you could be sharing a room in a youth hostel with people that you have never met before. That's life on the road! If you don't like the sound of it, there are lots of other jobs out there!

6 Follow the instructions and play the game with a partner.

1. Choose six words for things. They could be food, animals, places, objects, etc. Write definitions.

   This is a fruit that is long and yellow.

2. Choose four words for people. They could be jobs, members of the family or roles. Don't choose individuals or fictional characters. Write definitions.

   This is a person who comes from the US.

3. Now read your definitions to your partner. Did he or she guess your definitions on the first try?

   I know! It's a banana!

4. At the end, count how many words your partner guessed correctly. Did he or she get six out of six?

   Is it an American?

Reading & Writing

1 Complete the article with the letters of the missing sentences.

a. Instead, he works with a large team of people.
b. He hasn't always been a successful artist.
c. His next project will probably look at technology.
d. Is it just a clever trick?
e. China has a history of art going back thousands of years.
f. They often require around ten hours of makeup.
g. So far, he has "disappeared" into many famous buildings like Beijing's Olympic Stadium.

The Invisible Man
Liu Bolin

BY Roberta Ward

Now you see him, now you don't! Liu Bolin is the invisible man, an artist who disappears into the background of his pictures. (1) ☐ Now, Liu Bolin and other Chinese artists like Ai Weiwei are continuing that tradition. Forget Paris and New York; the new center of the art world is Beijing. Liu is a photographer who **disguises** his face and body, so that it is almost impossible to see him in pictures. (2) ☐ He also uses iconic images like London's red telephone boxes. However, his most impressive photos are when he hides in everyday places like a comic shop or the fruit **shelves** at a supermarket. So why did Liu Bolin become the invisible man? (3) ☐ In fact, he has a real artistic objective. Liu is showing how people who live in cities feel. Many people in modern cities feel small next to the enormous skyscrapers that are appearing all around them. We all become invisible in these situations. Liu's art also comes from his personal experience. (4) ☐ When he left art school, he was **unemployed**. He felt invisible because he had no role in society. This was a major inspiration in his work. This art involves hard work. It takes an enormous amount of time to prepare each photograph. (5) ☐ The final result is spectacular. Many people who are in the area when he is taking his photos don't even realize that Liu is there. Like many modern artists, Liu doesn't work alone. (6) ☐ This includes a number of different assistants. There are makeup artists who paint his clothes and body, as well as photographers who take the final picture. However, Bolin paints his clothes himself first, and then gives instructions to his helpers while they are working. He's almost like a film director.
What is the future for Liu Bolin? (7) ☐ For many young people today, it is impossible to disappear. We are visible all the time online, on Facebook and other websites. He is now thinking about our relationship with the online world and how it is watching us every minute of the day. Whatever artwork he creates, we can be sure that Liu Bolin won't be the invisible man any more.

Stop and Think! How does Liu Bolin express passion for what he does? Does he **convey** a message through his work?

2 Circle T (True) or F (False).

1. Liu Bolin is the only major artist now working in China. T F
2. He only takes photographs in Asia. T F
3. His art explores how people in urban areas feel. T F
4. He was very successful at the beginning of his career. T F
5. He is always silent when he is preparing his photos. T F
6. He now wants to look at people and the Internet. T F

Be Strategic!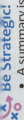

- A summary is a short explanation of a text.
- It is usually about one paragraph long.
- It is usually in the present tense.

E.g., The article discusses working from home.

- In the first line of your summary, explain the main point of the text. What is it about? What is its message?

E.g., This article describes a common medical problem. This text explains what happens when people travel by helicopter.

- Do not include sentences from the original article in your summary. Use your own words.
- In a summary, show that you are describing the opinions of another author. A summary does not include your own opinion.

Glossary

disguise: to change how you look so people don't recognize you

shelf (shelves): a flat piece of wood or metal that you put things on

unemployed: when you want a job but you don't have one

convey: to make (something) known to someone

---

3 Read the definition of a summary in the *Be Strategic!* section. Then underline useful key words to remember.

4 Read the examples of sentences from a summary and underline the verbs used in each one.

The author argues that electric cars are the vehicle of the future.
Dr. Murphy shows that the world of work is changing all the time.
The report states that the problem is a serious one.
The author reveals that there will be big changes in the future.

5 🎧 40 Number the sentences to complete a summary of Liu Bolin's article. Then listen and check.

☐ Liu Bolin makes photographs where he disappears into the background.
☐ He works with a team of makeup artists and photographers to create the final image.
☐ According to Liu Bolin, people feel small in today's cities, as if they are invisible.
☐ These people work for about 10 hours on each image.
☐ Finally, Ward reveals that Liu is preparing new projects which will look at the Internet.
☐ This article discusses the work of Chinese artist Liu Bolin.
☐ Ward also explains how Liu makes his photos.
☐ The author, Roberta Ward, argues that these photos show how people feel in modern cities.

6 ⏱ 2 min **Think Fast!** Name as many artists as you know. They can be from the past, too.

7 Now write a summary of a text from another unit. Follow the steps.

1. Choose a text from an earlier reading or culture section. Read the text carefully.
2. Read the text again. Underline important information to include in your summary.
3. Write your summary. Remember to write only one paragraph.
4. State the main idea in your first sentence. Use the verbs from Activities 4 and 5.
5. Look again at your summary. Is there too much information?

Is there anything you can cut?

Culture

1 🎧⁴¹ **Circle the correct options to complete the text. Then listen and check.**

Alaska is the (1) **most crowded / biggest** state in the US. The capital is (2) **Juneau / Anchorage**. The name Alaska means "that which the (3) **wind / sea** breaks against." The US purchased Alaska from (4) **Russia / Denmark** in 1867. Alaska's native population include Eskimos, Indians and Aleuts. (5) **Two / Five** percent of the state is covered by glaciers. If you ever go to Alaska, you might be lucky enough to watch one crash into the ocean. The Bering Sea is one of the world's (6) **most / least** productive fishing grounds, producing huge quantities of King crab, salmon and other varieties of fish.

Bering Sea

Dutch Harbor

Guess What! The Discovery Channel started a documentary-style show in 2005 that shows the drama behind the crabbing industry in Alaska. It's called *Deadliest Catch* and it has 12 seasons!

2 Discuss the questions with a partner.
1. Have you ever heard of king **crab** fishing in Alaska?
2. Do you think it is a risky job?
3. What jobs are dangerous or **life-threatening**?

Stop and Think! Is it worth risking your life for a job that pays well?

3 Label the text with the correct headings in the box.

Crabs   Fishing   Hazards   Boats

One of the Deadliest Jobs – King Crab Fishing in Alaska

1 _____

Would you apply for one of the most dangerous jobs in the world? You would have to go to Alaska to fish for king crabs.
The season is short–it lasts only about four weeks during the months of October and January. When the crabbing season starts, around 250 boats depart from Dutch Harbor in the Bering Sea. The crew in each boat consists of one captain and three to nine deckhands, depending on the size of the boat. It's very difficult to locate where crabs are, so the captain's intuition and experience are crucial. The fishermen use 300-kilo traps called "**pots**" with **baits** of sardines and other fish which are dropped 200 meters deep into the ocean to catch king crabs. The pots are left below the ocean from five to 24 hours; however, some of them are lost in the ocean. There can be as many as 50 abandoned pots per square kilometer!

2 _____

Crabbing is not only a dangerous task, but it is also an exciting competition among boats. The bigger boats have the advantage of having bigger decks that carry more pots, so they can accumulate more crab before having to stop to off-load, and they have bigger crews to fish more pots in less time. The first to catch their first 45,000 kilos of crab in the least number of pots is the winner.

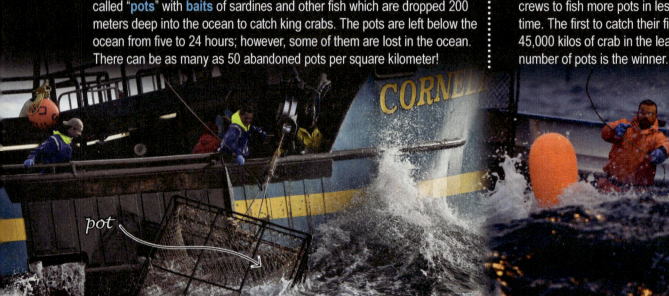

pot

4 Write the correct letter of the missing clauses.

1. The king crab season, ☐, takes place in the Bering Sea.
2. The pots, ☐, are dropped deep into the ocean.
3. Only the largest crabs, ☐, are fished.
4. The bigger boats, ☐, fish more pots.
5. Crab fishing in Alaska, ☐, is a very dangerous job.

a. which are male
b. which has the highest mortality rate
c. which lasts a few weeks
d. which weigh 300 kilos
e. which have bigger decks

5 Read the job ad. In your notebook, make a list of the pros and cons.

Experienced King Crabber Needed

Location: The Bering Sea in Alaska
Crabbing Season: October to January
Shift: A regular shift in a crabber's day is 21 hours long lifting pots out of the water in freezing temperatures.
Salary: From $60,000 to $100,000 in a season
Comments: You are expected to purchase your own wet-weather gear. Commercial fishing license required.

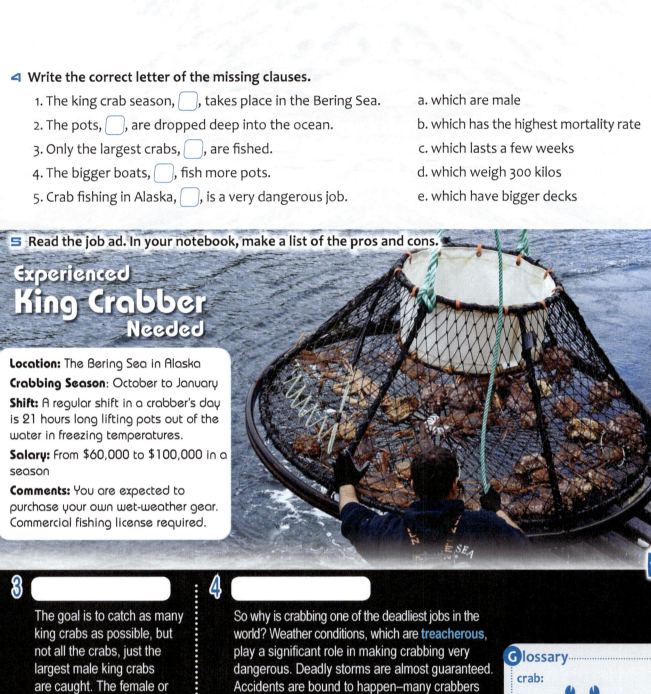

3 _____

The goal is to catch as many king crabs as possible, but not all the crabs, just the largest male king crabs are caught. The female or younger crabs are discarded and this results in injured crabs that in turn become bait for other crabs.

4 _____

So why is crabbing one of the deadliest jobs in the world? Weather conditions, which are **treacherous**, play a significant role in making crabbing very dangerous. Deadly storms are almost guaranteed. Accidents are bound to happen–many crabbers who fish in Alaska **drown** because they fall overboard. They might also be in a boat accident or die from hypothermia. These are the reasons why this occupation has the highest mortality rate. If you have a sense of adventure, crabbing in Alaska may be an option for you because it's not a common 9 to 5 job in an office. Would you apply for this job in spite of the risks involved?

Glossary

crab: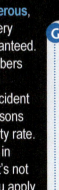

life-threatening: something that puts your life in danger

pot: a container that is used for storing or holding something

bait: something (such as a piece of food) that is used to attract fish or animals so they can be caught

treacherous: very dangerous and difficult to deal with

drown: to die by being underwater too long and unable to breathe

Project

1 Complete the survey about you.

	Completely agree 5	Partly agree 4	No strong opinion 3	Partly disagree 2	Completely disagree 1
1. I am very strong and fit.	○	○	○	○	○
2. I like games like chess and puzzles like Sudoku.	○	○	○	○	○
3. I know how to cook.	○	○	○	○	○
4. I have a great sense of direction. I never get lost.	○	○	○	○	○
5. I like to stay at home. I'm an indoors person.	○	○	○	○	○
6. I like to sing or act in the theater.	○	○	○	○	○
7. I often tell jokes with my friends.	○	○	○	○	○
8. I find it difficult to make decisions.	○	○	○	○	○
9. I'm not afraid of animals like spiders, snakes or dogs.	○	○	○	○	○
10. I'm a good member of a team. I like to listen to others.	○	○	○	○	○
11. I am good with my hands and I like making things.	○	○	○	○	○
12. I like to explore and visit new places.	○	○	○	○	○

2 Work in groups. Compare your answers to Activity 1 and discuss the questions.

1. Who is most similar to you?
2. Do you have any 5s that nobody else has?

3 In groups, read the situation and discuss the questions.

1. Where is the best place to build your village on the map? Mark it.
2. What are the advantages and disadvantages of the place you chose?

> There has been a disaster on Earth and you and your group are all alone. You need to make a new tribe to survive. You live in the place on the map. You have no towns, shops, companies, families or friends. You have the chance to create your own society. You are a tribe.

Stop and Think! Is there a possibility nowadays to cause the extinction of humankind? What could cause it?

4 **Now, you will get ready to assign jobs in your tribe. First, look at the jobs below and rank them from 1 (most important) to 8 (least important).**

Name

☐ A person who protects the tribe from wild animals or other possible tribes.
☐ A person who builds homes for the tribe.
☐ A person who tells stories and entertains the tribe.
☐ A person who gets water for the tribe.
☐ A person who cooks for the tribe.
☐ A person who paints the tribe's home and makes it look nice.
☐ A person who leads the tribe.
☐ A person who finds food for the tribe.

5 **Assign jobs in your tribe. Follow the steps.**
   1. Use your answers in Activity 1 to identify each person's talents.
   2. Assign the jobs. Write each person's name next to the jobs in Activity 4.
   3. If there are fewer than eight people in your group, do not fill the less important roles.

6 **In groups, discuss the questions.**
   1. Does everybody in the tribe agree with their jobs?
   2. Did two people want the same job? How did you solve it?
   3. What is your plan to survive?
   4. What will you do about the crocodile and the lion?
   5. Do you think your tribe will survive?

Review

1 Number the pictures that are related to each job below.

1. animation director
2. chef
3. sports coach
4. computer game programmer
5. crime scene investigator
6. graffiti artist
7. marine biologist
8. travel writer

2 Complete the dialogues with the jobs in Activity 1.

1. **A:** You were losing at halftime. How did you win the game?
   B: Our _____ gave a great team talk and told us we were winners. It worked!

2. **A:** My dad is in the Gulf of California in Mexico at the moment. He's a _____ and he studies gray whales.
   B: Wow! What a job!

3. **A:** What does an _____ do?
   B: They manage the people who make the animations and they also tell the actors what to do on set.

4. **A:** Hmm, this lasagna tastes delicious! Who cooked it?
   B: I did. My aunt showed me. She's a _____ in an Italian restaurant.

5. **A:** Something's wrong with my laptop! It's not working.
   B: I'll ask my sister to look at it. She's a _____. She knows everything about computers!

6. **A:** How come you have all these guidebooks in your bedroom: Colombia, Australia, the US, Europe?
   B: I want to be a _____ when I finish school, so I'm reading the books to learn how to do it.

7. **A:** Who painted those amazing pictures on the school wall?
   B: A _____. The school principal asked him to do it.

8. **A:** Did you see that murder mystery on TV last night?
   B: Yeah! It was fascinating. When I grow up, I want to be a _____ like the detective on the show.

3 Complete the missing letters.

1. Chefs often work l___ ___g hours. They often don't finish until midnight.
2. My grandpa is 59 and he wants to r___t___r___, but he can't stop working yet. He has to wait until he's 65.
3. I have a new job! I'm signing the c___ ___ tr___ ___t today.
4. Salespeople often e___ ___n a lot of money, but they travel a lot.
5. I can't get a good job because I didn't study and I don't have any q___al___f___ ___at___ ___ns.
6. I want to be a marine biologist. I'm going to ap___l___ for a place to get work experience with some scientists this summer.
7. My mom is a company director. She m___n___g___s a team of a hundred people.
8. If you work for a telephone help desk, you d___ ___l with problems from the general public.

4 Complete the text with *who* or *which*.

Ryan Germick is a man (1) _____ has changed your life. You might not know his name, but you have seen his work. He's an art director (2) _____ chooses the Google Doodles. Google Doodles are the images (3) _____ appear on the Google home page. They celebrate different things, like famous people (4) _____ have an anniversary that day (a birth or a death). Ryan doesn't work alone. There are ten artists (5) _____ he manages. They have designed games like the Pacman Doodle (6) _____ people played on their computers. Their programmers can design instruments (7) _____ you can use to play music, like the one for the anniversary of Robert Moog, the inventor of the synthesizer.

Germick also works with local experts (8) _____ help him create doodles for every country in the world. There are always cultural differences (9) _____ can cause problems, so Germick and his team check all their Doodles carefully before they go online.

And what is Germick's own favorite? A video about Charlie Chaplin (10) _____ stars Germick as a police officer. He is truly a man who lives his job.

5 Add commas around the non-defining relative clauses. Mark (✓) the correct sentences.

1. ☐ There are a lot of people who work in shops helping customers find what they want.
2. ☐ My mom who works for the police is a crime scene investigator.
3. ☐ My friend Sam is a chef and he gave me a recipe for green curry which comes from Thailand.
4. ☐ Our sports coach who we really like is leaving the school.
5. ☐ Ellie is a computer game programmer which is a cool job.

Just for Fun

1 Complete the crossword puzzle.

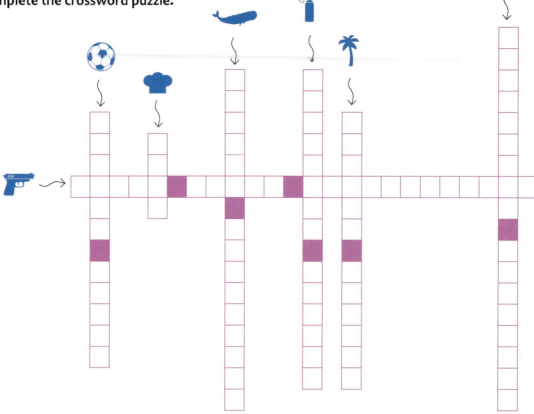

2 Complete the sentences with the people's names.

1. _____ is the first woman to be appointed as the White House Executive Chef since 2005. Michelle Obama, who asked her to stay, loved her creativity and healthy cooking.

2. _____, who studied character animation, is a writer and movie director. He has won two Oscar Awards for Best Animated Feature for *Wall·E* and *Finding Nemo*. His latest movie is *Finding Dory*.

3. _____ worked for Google and has been the Chief Executive Officer of YouTube since 2014. She is a successful executive who also manages to be a happy mom of five children.

4. _____ is the host of a TV show called *Street Food Around the World*. In each episode the host, who is Israeli, walks the streets of different places and tastes food that locals like.

Cristeta Comerford

Andrew Stanton

Ishai Golan

Susan Wojcick

Unit 1

Vocabulary – Types of Music and Adjectives

1 Write the music category. There are three extra.

> country   classical   Latin   jazz   world music   pop   rap   ~~reggae~~   rock

0. Jamaica / Bob Marley / drums / bass — _reggae_
1. saxophone / Louis Armstrong / New Orleans, LA / trumpet — _____
2. banjo / Nashville, TN / cowboy boots / guitar — _____
3. Julio Iglesias / Spanish and Portuguese / Salsa / Bachata — _____
4. violin / orchestra / conductor / Beethoven — _____
5. Michael Jackson / teenagers / Justin Bieber / dance — _____

2 Correct the mistake in each sentence.

> dramatic   catchy   relaxing   moving   ~~loud~~   inspiring

0. <u>Inspiring</u> music sometimes hurts my ears. — _loud_
1. That song is so <u>relaxing</u>! I can always remember it and I have to sing along each time I hear it. — _____
2. I often listen to classical music before I go to bed. It's so <u>dramatic</u> that it helps me sleep. — _____
3. Movies often include orchestra music for its <u>catchy</u> scenes to make the viewer feel the action. — _____
4. The song "Imagine", by John Lennon, is all about world peace and how to achieve it. It's so <u>loud</u>! — _____
5. I think Latin music is the most <u>dramatic</u>. I always feel sad hearing about lost loves. — _____

3 Unscramble the words.

0. (zajz) _jazz_
1. (lacslicas) _____
2. (yuncotr) _____
3. (eggear) _____
4. (korc) _____
5. (par) _____

4 **Look and match.**

0. __e__ Amy is listening to loud music!
1. _____ The music Ben is listening to is very moving.
2. _____ Juan and Lily are listening to relaxing music.
3. _____ Sara likes catchy music. She always dances along.
4. _____ Many rock songs are very inspiring.
5. _____ This kind of music often accompanies ballets or plays to make them more dramatic.

Grammar – as ... as

1 **Read and mark the correct description.**

0. a. (Jill is as tall as her mom.)
   b. Jill isn't as tall as her mom.
1. a. Todd is as good at guitar as he is at drums.
   b. Todd isn't as good at guitar as he is at drums.
2. a. For Melody, math is as difficult as English.
   b. For Melody, math isn't as difficult as English.
3. a. Jeff thinks a hamburger is as good as a salad.
   b. Jeff thinks a hamburger isn't as good as a salad.
4. a. Duncan isn't as old as Sam.
   b. Duncan is as old as Sam.
5. a. My dog isn't as big as yours.
   b. My dog is as big as yours.

2 **Write the sentences.**

0. bears / elephants / big — _Bears are not as big as elephants._
1. mother / grandmother / old — _____
2. I / my twin brother / old — _____
3. a whisper / a shout / loud — _____
4. junk food / a salad / good for you — _____
5. soccer / basketball / competitive — _____

Unit 1

Gerunds and Nouns

3 Read and circle the correct gerund or noun.

0. (Dancing) / Listening to music is great exercise! It really gets you moving.
1. **Rock** / **Classical music** is usually played loud.
2. **Playing** / **Singing** the guitar is really fun.
3. **The band** / **The orchestra** at school usually plays classical music.
4. **The drums** / **The bass** is a stringed instrument.
5. **Ice skating** / **Reading** is beautiful to watch.

4 Read and underline the gerund or noun. Then match.

0. Rap is a lot like poetry. — e. The rhythm is very important.
1. Singing is important in most types of music.   a. People listen to it all over the world.
2. Playing the drums relieves stress.   b. It takes real skill and talent.
3. Reggae is from Jamaica.   c. I often do it when I need a release.
4. Rock is so popular.   d. It's a small island in the Caribbean.
5. Dancing is an art.   f. Almost all bands have vocals.

5 Read and fill in the blanks to express your opinion.

0. Swimming is as ___fun___ as ___basketball___.
1. Rap is as _____ as _____.
2. Chemistry isn't as _____ as _____.
3. The band is as _____ as the _____.
4. World music is as _____ as _____.
5. Classical music isn't as _____ as _____.

Review

1 Write sentences using a word from each column.

| jazz, world music, Latin, rap, pop, country, reggae, rock, classical | is / isn't | as... | relaxing, dramatic, catchy, inspiring, loud | as... |

0. In my opinion, rock music is as catchy as pop.
1. _____.
2. _____.
3. _____.
4. _____.
5. _____.

HOW TO START A BAND

Reading

1 Read the article and label each section.

- Play live shows and record
- Interview
- ~~Brainstorm~~
- Practice
- Most importantly, enjoy
- Advertise
- Market your band

Have you always wanted to start a band but don't know where to begin? Well, I have some tips for you on how to begin and how to get noticed.

0. _____Brainstorm_____: Think about the type of music you want to play and the types of instruments used. Is it rock, pop, country or another genre?

1. _____: Put up flyers or post on your Facebook page. Tell others you are looking to start a band and list the specific musicians you are looking for.

2. _____: Meet with the people who are interested in participating. Choose people that you think would be a good fit.

3. _____: Find a place that is accessible for everyone and get together often and practice a lot! During these sessions you will also be "finding your sound" and making an image for yourself.

4. _____: Once you and your band members feel you have made progress, it's time to show what you've got to an audience. Talk to local venues (places to play) as well as recording studios.

5. _____: Tell everyone you know about your band! Advertise your shows and records. Create a website or Facebook page.

6. _____: After all, you are playing music because you love it. Don't forget to have fun!

2 Read the article again and circle *T* (True) or *F* (False).

0. Having fun is not the most important part.   T   (F)
1. You shouldn't tell everyone about your band.   T   F
2. It's important to think about the instruments needed.   T   F
3. Play your songs over and over again until you master them.   T   F
4. Facebook is not a good way to advertise your band.   T   F

Writing

3 Use the ideas below to write about a band you would like to start.

1. Type of band
2. Kinds of instruments
3. How to advertise for members
4. Where to play
5. Practice details
6. Marketing your band

Unit 2

Vocabulary – Life Experiences

1 Categorize the words in the box in the correct activity.

> tent   haircut   ~~software~~   photos   sheet music   cook stove
> makeup   rehearsals   saddle   identification   carrying case
> suitcase   costume   reins   compass   life jacket

0. Design your own web page — _software_
1. Camp overnight
2. Travel by plane
3. Perform in a play
4. Sail a boat
5. Learn to play a musical instrument
6. Change your look
7. Ride a horse

Guess What! 27% of teens maintain their own web page.

2 Match the underlined mistake to its correction.

0. Ben loves animals, so he wants to change his look.
1. My best friend can design her own web page because she loves the water.
2. I've always wanted to perform in a play so I can see Asia.
3. My cousin said she needed a new start, so she's going to ride a horse.
4. My friends and I love the outdoors, so we want to learn to play a musical instrument.
5. I love graphic art and surfing the Internet. I'll travel by plane.
6. My mom plays the violin and wants me to ride like her.
7. I love acting and being in front of an audience. I will sail a boat.

a. learn to play a musical instrument
b. camp overnight
c. design my own web page
d. ride a horse
e. sail a boat
f. travel by plane
g. perform in a play
h. change her look

3 Complete the sentences with the words in the box.

> camp overnight   change your look   ~~design your own web page~~   travel by plane
> sail a boat   ride a horse   perform in a play

0. If you want to promote your family's business, you can _design your own website_.
1. Yosemite is a great national park where you can _____.
2. I'm in the acting club this year because I've always wanted to _____.
3. There are some great trails near my house where you can _____.
4. To get from the US to Japan you can take a boat or _____.
5. You could get a haircut and buy some new clothes to _____.
6. My dad loves being on the water, so he will teach me to _____.

Your own web page

Set up your profile! Let your readers know a little about you.

Grammar – Present Perfect

1 Read and circle the correct option.

My name is Emily and I started this web page to let everyone at our school know about the excellent athletics program and report on news and events for athletes at our school. Maybe you didn't know, but we have over 10 sports teams! I (0) **have** / **has** participated in three teams myself. In fact, I've been a member of the soccer team (1) **since** / **for** I was in elementary school. I also (2) **play** / **played** volleyball. Our team (3) **won** / **has won** three championships since the program started two years ago. I also love to travel. My family and I (4) **went** / **have been** to New York last year. We were there (5) **since** / **for** two weeks. I (6) **has** / **have** been to Europe, too! My classmates and I (7) **have been** / **went** on a tour together a few months ago. It was amazing! Well, that's a little bit about me. It's nice to meet you and I hope you enjoy my web page!

2 Look and complete the sentences with what the person has or hasn't done.

Mike (travel by plane) _Mike has traveled by plane_.

Steve (perform in a play) _____.

Sam and her family (camp) _____.

Marcela (play the guitar) _____.

Robert (ride a horse) _____.

Unit

3 Complete the conversation with *for* or *since*.

JASON: Hi, Jen! I saw the article in the school paper about you. It was great!

JEN: Thanks, Jason.

JASON: I didn't know you rode a horse. How long have you been riding?

JEN: I've been riding (0) __for__ five years, (1) _____ I was 10 years old.

JASON: Cool. I rode a horse once, but it was scary! And you have your own web page, too! How long have you had it?

JEN: I've had the page up (2) _____ about six months.

JASON: That's so cool! And you are in the computer club, too? How long have you been a member?

JEN: I've been a member (3) _____ 2013. And what about you? How long have you wanted to be a reporter?

JASON: Ha ha! I do ask a lot of questions. I've wanted to join the paper (4) _____ a year. I'm finally going to apply next semester!

Review

1 Make sentences about your experiences with the words in the box.

ride a horse   sail a boat   camp overnight   learn to play a musical instrument
travel by plane   change my look   design my own web page   perform in an play

I've done it. / When?	I haven't done it.
I've ridden a horse. I rode one last year.	I haven't sailed a boat.

132

Reading

1 Complete the article with the correct headings.

a. Promote your web page
b. ~~Decide on a web host and a domain name~~
c. Test your web page
d. Design your web page.

HOW TO CREATE YOUR OWN WEB PAGE

Have you always been interested in starting your own web page? Maybe you want to promote your family's business or maybe you just want to start blogging. Here are some very easy steps you can take to get started.

0. _Decide on a web host and a domain name_
A web host is basically the website that will get you connected. It's a company that has many computers **hooked up** to the Internet and your web page will be on one of them. The domain name is the name you want for your site. You have to make sure it's not already taken. Some hosts charge a small fee. One good site with reasonable fees is GoDaddy.com©. If you aren't able to pay, a good option is Wordpress.com©. You have to register with any company you choose.

1. _____
As you do this, you will have to think about two main parts: content and layout. _Content_ refers to the information you will put on the site. Will you have links to other sites on it or videos, perhaps? It's all up to what you want to include. _Layout_ is how you will arrange the content on the web page including placement, colors and design. You will want to think about color schemes, sequencing of information and graphics you will include.

2. _____
Right after you have the "rough draft" of your web page, you will want to test it on all major **Internet browsers**. All are available for free download. If you have a smartphone, try it out there, too! Does the web page look the way you want it to or do you need to make changes?

3. _____
In addition to telling family and friends about your site, you can submit it to search engines like Google© and Bing© so that it will appear when someone does a search for it. You can also promote your site the old fashioned way, by word of mouth, advertisements in newspapers or by handing out flyers. Now that you have your web page, you have to get the word out.

2 Correct the false information in the sentences.

0. GoDaddy© is a free web host while WordPress© charges a fee.
   WordPress© is a free web host while GoDaddy© charges a fee.

1. _Layout_ refers to the specific information you chose to include on your web page.
   _____

2. It doesn't matter if you have the same domain name as another web page.
   _____

3. Designing your own web page is always complicated. You need to be a programmer.
   _____

Writing

3 In your notebook, complete the outline below. Then write your plan to design your own web page.

- Name of my web page
- Web page host
- Major content to include
- Layout ideas
- Where to promote my site

Glossary

hook up: to connect

Internet browser: also web browser, the software that allows the user to access the Internet

Unit 3

Vocabulary – Phrasal Verbs

1 Write the words in the correct column.

the closet   your coat   these shoes   the dishes   the old newspaper
the cabinet   the mirror   the laundry   your shirts   the groceries

pick up	throw away	put away	clean out	hang up
			the closet	

2 Correct the phrasal verb.

0. How many times have I asked you to <u>throw away</u> your books?!   _put away_
1. On Sunday, let's make some time to <u>wipe up</u> the closets.   _____
2. I always <u>pick up</u> my keys when I get home so I don't lose them.   _____
3. I hate to <u>hang up</u> food. It's such a waste!   _____
4. In *The Karate Kid*, the boy gets a lesson in how to <u>wash up</u> his coat.   _____
5. It's my sister's job to to <u>put away</u> the trash.   _____

3 Label the pictures with the correct phrasal verb.

throw away

4 **Match the sentence halves.**

0. Jimmy, please wipe off
1. Can you please put away
2. Don't throw away
3. Don't forget to hang up your pants
4. Pick up your shoes
5. Today you are going to clean out

a. that box! Recycle it!
b. the table so we can eat dinner.
c. your closet. Your new clothes don't even fit in it.
d. so they don't get wrinkled.
e. off the floor, please.
f. your books? They go on the shelf!

Grammar – Past Perfect

1 **Look at the pictures and mark (✓) the sentences that might be true.**

We went out of town for the weekend and left our teenage daughter alone.
We thought we could trust her!

0. When we got back she had had a party. ✓
1. She had invited lots of friends. ____
2. She hadn't folded her clothes. ____
3. She had washed up the dishes. ____
4. She had been very responsible. ____
5. She hadn't ordered pizza. ____

Unit 3

2 Read and rewrite the actions that Debbie had completed by the time her mom got home from work.

Good morning, Debbie. I have to go to work today. I know it's Saturday! Here is your schedule for the day. Please be sure and get everything done on time!

9:00 a.m. – wake up
9:15 a.m. – have breakfast
10:00 a.m. – clean your room
10:30 a.m. – take a break
11:00 a.m. – do your homework
1:00 p.m. – pick up your little brother from camp
2:00 p.m. – go to the grocery store
3:00 p.m. – start making dinner

I'll be home by 4:00 p.m. I love you!

0. Debbie had woken up.
1. _____
2. _____
3. _____
4. _____
5. _____
6. _____
7. _____

3 Look at the picture and complete the sentences with the past perfect.

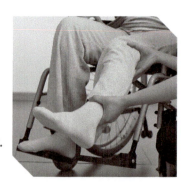

0. Maybe he ____had fallen____ (fall) while working.
1. Maybe his experiment _____ (go) wrong.
2. Maybe he _____ (be) in a car accident.
3. Maybe he _____ (broke) his leg.
4. Maybe his little brother _____ (hit) him accidentally.
5. Maybe he _____ (got) hurt playing soccer.

Review

1 Complete the e-mail with the past perfect of the verbs in parentheses.

To: Carmen
Cc:
Subject: Kevin's birthday party

Hi Carmen!

Guess what? Yesterday my roommates and I decided to have a surprise birthday party for Kevin. I had to work at the bookstore, so I couldn't help much. When I got there at six o'clock they (0) __had picked up__ (pick up) all the mess on the floor like our shoes and books. They (1) _____ (wipe off) the table. They (2) _____ (take out) the trash and (3) _____ (hang up) balloons to decorate and (4) _____ (buy) a birthday cake, too! By the time I got there, all I could do was join in the party!

Becky

Reading

1 Read the article. Then write K (Karla) or J (Jenessa).

Point – Counterpoint: Should teenagers be paid an allowance for doing chores?

Point: I believe that it is important to pay teenagers an **allowance** for doing their chores. It teaches them responsibility and ensures that they help around the house. It shouldn't only be the parent's job to cook and clean. Teens should help out too and paying them an allowance will encourage them to do so.
Paying teens an allowance for chores also teaches them the value of money. They can learn about savings and managing their money which will better prepare them for independence in the future. It's essential!

Counterpoint: I think it's OK to give teens an allowance, but it should not be tied to the chores they do. Teens should be required to pitch in and help around the house, not **bribed** to do so. It is their responsibility as a member of the family and they should do certain chores like washing up dishes, putting away groceries or taking out the trash even without the promise of money.
Perhaps some chores could be rewarded with a **monetary** benefit like cutting the grass or painting the house. That would recognize a teen going above and beyond the expectations set by the family, but just for cleaning their room? No way!

0. __K__ Parents are not the only ones who should be responsible for cooking.
1. ____ Allowing teens to earn money through chores will teach them the value of money.
2. ____ Teens should be paid an allowance for some chores, beyond just cleaning their room.
3. ____ Paying teens for doing chores will make sure that they help out around the house.
4. ____ Teens should be expected to help at home, not paid to do so.

Writing

2 Read the article again and answer the questions.

1. What is Karla's strongest argument for paying teens an allowance for doing chores?

    _____

2. What is Jenessa's strongest argument for why teens should not be given an allowance for doing chores?

    _____

3 In your notebook, write your own opinion about the article.

Make sure to include:
- Which author do you most agree with and why?
- Would you give your own children an allowance for doing chores? Why or why not?

Glossary

allowance: a sum of money given to a person on a regular basis for general expenses

bribe: to give money or any other valuable to persuade a person to do something

monetary: relating to money

Unit 4

Vocabulary – Adverbs of Manner and Superstitions

1 Label the pictures with the words in the box.

> fortune cookie   four-leaf clover   ladybug   evil eye
> horseshoe   rabbit's foot   ~~fortune cat~~

0. fortune cat

2 Match the underlined words or phrases to the correct adverbs with a similar meaning.

0. We got to Ben's party <u>fast</u>. — a. slowly
1. Kelly spilled her juice <u>without meaning to</u>. — b. stupidly
2. I always tell my mom to walk <u>not so fast</u>. — c. accidentally
3. My dad sings, but <u>not very well</u>. — d. quickly
4. <u>I wasn't thinking and</u> left my keys in the fridge! — e. badly

3 Underline the adverbs. Then write the correct adjective forms.

0. It was a difficult situation, but you handled it <u>cleverly</u>.   clever
1. I saw you deliberately hit your little brother!   _____
2. Cats walk silently so they can attack their prey.   _____
3. My teacher speaks so quickly that I have trouble understanding her.   _____
4. I accidentally dropped my favorite **mug** and broke it.   _____

4 Correct the mistakes.

0. Is Jill a good driver?
I don't think so. She drives too ~~accidentally~~.
_____quickly_____

1. How did your sister sing in the recital?
She sang silently. I felt bad for her.
_____

2. Could you hear the announcement?
No, she spoke too deliberately.
_____

3. Did the students listen respectfully to the speaker?
No, they talked quickly during his presentation.
_____

4. What did Ben do when you spilled your drink?
He badly grabbed a towel to wipe it up.
_____

Grammar – The Second Conditional

1 Write commas (,) where needed.

0. If people drove more carefully, there would be fewer accidents.
1. I wouldn't get better grades if I studied more.
2. We would win more games if we practiced soccer more.
3. If I did my homework more quickly I would have more time to watch TV.
4. If Jenny lost her rabbit's foot she would have good luck.

2 Match the sentence halves.

0. If I found someone's wallet on the street,   a. if my dog chewed it.
1. I would invite my friends from school and from my neighborhood   b. I would make a wish.
2. If my teacher was sick,   c. I wouldn't take it.
3. If I saw a **shooting star**,   d. if I threw a party.
4. I would have to do my homework again   e. we would have a substitute.

3 Complete the second conditional sentences with the correct form of the words in parentheses.

0. I ___would have___ (have) good luck if I ___found___ (find) a four-leaf clover.
1. If my parents _____ (win) the lottery, they _____ (be) worried about money.
2. I _____ (be) so happy if my fortune cookie _____ (say) my dreams will come true.
3. If I _____ (break) a mirror, I _____ (have) seven years of bad luck!
4. If the government _____ (give) free college tuition to everyone, I _____ (have) to pay!

Glossary

mug:

shooting star: a meteor that lights up when it enters Earth's atmosphere

Unit 4

4 Use the prompts to make second conditional sentences that are true for you.

0. win a million dollars / buy
   If I won a million dollars, I would buy a new house for my family.

1. fail a test / my parents
   _____

2. my best friend move away / I
   _____

3. my teacher catch me cheating / not
   _____

4. can do whatever I want / I
   _____

5. play music loudly / my neighbors
   _____

Review

1 Complete the second conditional sentences.

0. If I found a four-leaf clover, *I would give it to my sister*.
1. If my fortune cookie said I would live forever, _____.
2. If I had a time machine, _____.
3. If a ladybug landed on my hand, _____.
4. If I accidentally broke a glass in a store, _____.

Reading

1 Read the article about superstitions.

෴ Strange Superstitions ෴

A superstition is belief that is not based on human reason or scientific knowledge, but is connected with old ideas about magic. Do you avoid walking under a ladder or believe that if you break a mirror you will have seven years of bad luck?

1 See a penny, pick it up? Of course! Who doesn't like free money? In ancient times, people thought that if you found a coin, it was a gift from the gods that would protect you from evil. Nowadays, many people believe that a penny found heads-up is extra lucky. So grab those pennies!

2 Don't open an umbrella indoors? Common sense tells us that opening an umbrella indoors is a bad idea. You can poke someone's eye out or break a fragile object! The origin of this superstition is unknown, but some say it was an insult to the sun gods and others say it originated in Victorian England.

3 Throw salt over your shoulder? This superstition comes from the idea that the devil is always standing behind your left shoulder and throwing salt in his eyes will distract him from the trouble he causes. But only do it when you accidentally spill salt.

4 Say "God bless you" after someone sneezes? Have you ever noticed almost everyone seems **compelled** to bless you after you sneeze, even total strangers? This superstition originates from the time of the **bubonic plague**. It was thought to protect against the spreading of the disease. Other explanations are that the soul escapes during a sneeze or that the heart momentarily stops beating so the blessing welcomed the person back to life. In other cultures, the **utterance** is thought to bring good luck.

2 Read the article again and write the correct number of the superstition.

3 Read the article again and circle *T* (True) or *F* (False).

0. Picking up a tails-up penny is extra good luck. T (F)
1. Opening an umbrella inside will bring good luck to the person. T F
2. People believe that throwing salt in the devil's eye will poison him. T F
3. Saying "God bless you" after someone sneezes comes from the time of the bubonic plague. T F
4. People used to believe that the soul left the body when someone sneezed. T F

Writing

4 In your notebook, write an opinion essay about superstitions. Follow the guidelines below.

- Paragraph 1: Introduce the topic of superstitions and write your thesis statement. This sentence states if you are for or against superstitions.
- Paragraph 2: Describe the differences in your culture with the superstitions in the article. Write if you believe them and if you follow them.
- Paragraph 3: Write about a superstition in your country. Describe it in detail.
- Paragraph 4: Write your conclusion about superstitions. Paraphrase your thesis statement. Explain why you are for or against superstitions.

Glossary

compelled: to feel forced to do something

bubonic plague: a plague that spread over Europe in the 14th century

utterance: a spoken word or statement

Unit 5

Vocabulary – Air travel

1 Match the phrases.

0. pick up — d. your luggage
1. land
2. print off
3. go through
4. book
5. board

a. the plane
b. your flight
c. at your destination
d. your luggage
e. your boarding pass
f. passport control

Guess What!
In 2015, nearly 3.6 billion people traveled by plane. That is 48% of the world's population!

2 Complete the e-mail with the words in the box.

arrive   go through (x2)   board   ~~book~~   pick up   check in
lands   takes off   print out

To: Lisa Taylor; Tom Williams; Alex Brown
Subject: My first flight

Hi everyone!
My family and I just got back from Rio de Janeiro, Brazil. It was the first time I had ever flown. It's very convenient because you can (0) ___book___ your flight online. Then you have to (1) _____ at the airport three hours early because it's an international flight. Once you get there, you (2) _____ your luggage and (3) _____ your boarding pass (or you can do this at home if you have a printer). Next you (4) _____ security and go to your gate. When they call your row number, you (5) _____ the plane. Probably the scariest part is when the plane (6) _____ because it can be a bit bumpy. The flight itself was not bad. I got free drinks and snacks and I even saw movies. Then before you know it, the plane (7) _____ at your destination. When you get off the plane, you have to (8) _____ your luggage and (9) _____ customs. Flying can be a long process, but it's worth it when you get to the beach!
Rick

Saved at 2:03 pm

Places

3 Write the names of the countries under the correct landmarks.

Brazil   Croatia   US   Spain   Italy   Mexico (x2)   ~~Peru~~

Machu Picchu
Peru

Chichén Itzá

Walls of Ston

Christ the Redeemer

Golden Gate

David

Palenque

Camp Nou

4 Write the landmarks in Activity 3 in the correct columns.

Walls	Statues	Pyramids	Bridges	Stadiums	Ruins
					Machu Picchu

Grammar – Preferences

1 Circle the correct options to complete the sentences.

0. **A:** Would you rather fly or take a train across Europe?

   B: I'd rather not / (rather) fly because a train would take too long.

1. **A:** I'd prefer to print out my boarding pass at home. How about you?

   B: I'd prefer / I'd rather to print it out at the airport because I don't have a printer at home.

2. **A:** What do you want to do today?

   B: I'm not sure if **I would like / I wouldn't like** to see the temple or the ruins.

3. **A:** Let's walk across the Golden Gate Bridge!

   B: I'd rather / I'd prefer not to because I'm afraid of heights.

4. **A:** Do you want to try bungee jumping?

   B: I'd prefer / I'd rather not. It looks scary!

5. **A:** Where should we go on our next vacation? How about the beach?

   B: I **would like / wouldn't like** to go there. I'd prefer to visit a city.

Unit 5

2 Complete the sentences with *too* or *enough*.

0. I didn't put on _____enough_____ sunblock, so I got sunburned!
1. My little brother is _____ short to ride the roller coaster at the amusement park.
2. Do we have _____ money for the hotel?
3. My mom spent _____ much time to get ready to go to the pool.
4. I don't think my dad has _____ time to book the flight.
5. I think you are never _____ young to travel. You can learn so much!

3 Rewrite the sentences exchanging *too* for *enough* and vice versa. The sentences should have the same meaning.

0. I'm too short! — I'm not tall enough.
1. She's not old enough. _____
2. It's too small. _____
3. The tea is too hot to drink. _____
4. He's not strong enough. _____
5. Is it late enough to call? _____

Review

1 Mark the sentences correct (✓) or incorrect (✗). Rewrite the incorrect sentences.

0. I would like to see the pyramids, but it's hot enough outside. [✗]
   I would like to see the pyramids, but it's too hot outside.
1. She'd prefer learn Spanish, but she doesn't have enough time. ☐
   _____
2. We'd rather take a taxi because the hotel is too far to walk. ☐
   _____
3. He doesn't have too experience to get the job. ☐
   _____
4. Matt would rather not go on the tour because he doesn't have enough money. ☐
   _____
5. I'd prefer not go to the ruins because it's raining. ☐
   _____

The Most Famous Walls in the World

The Wall of Troy is the one of the oldest walls in history, built in the 13th century BCE. It is over 4,000 years old! It is located in modern-day Turkey. It was so strong that it withstood the 10-year **siege** of the the Trojan War. The famous ancient author, Homer, wrote about the site in his epic poem *The Iliad*.

Hadrian's Wall was built in England in 122 AD during the reign of Emperor Hadrian as a defensive barricade. It was built by the Romans to protect their colony, Britannia, from attacks by Scottish tribes in the north. It marked the northern point of the Roman Empire and is the longest wall in Europe.

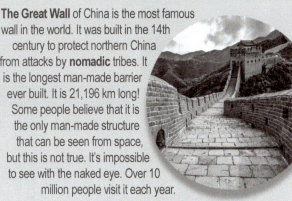

The Great Wall of China is the most famous wall in the world. It was built in the 14th century to protect northern China from attacks by **nomadic** tribes. It is the longest man-made barrier ever built. It is 21,196 km long! Some people believe that it is the only man-made structure that can be seen from space, but this is not true. It's impossible to see with the naked eye. Over 10 million people visit it each year.

The Western Wall is located in Israel and it is one of the most sacred places for Jewish people. It is one of the four walls where the holy Temple Mount stood. The wall was built in 19 BCE by Herod the Great. It was almost completely destroyed by Roman armies in 70 AD. It is a place of **pilgrimage** and one of the most visited sites in the ancient city of Jerusalem.

The Berlin Wall has a short but important history. It was built in 1961 and torn down in 1989. It was built during the time of the cold war to divide the communist East Germany from West Germany. East Germany constructed the wall to prevent movement and influence from the West whose political ideals it did not share. The wall was destroyed when East Germany was dissolved and the country reunited.

Reading

1 Match each wall with its location. Then read and check your answers.

0. Hadrian's Wall — c. England
1. Wall of Troy
2. Berlin Wall
3. Great Wall
4. Western Wall

a. Germany
b. China
c. England
d. Israel
e. Turkey

2 Read the text again and circle T (True) or F (False).

0. The Great Wall of China can be seen from space with the naked eye. T (F)
1. The Western Wall is important for Jewish people because it was the last piece of a holy temple that was left standing after the Roman invasion. T F
2. The Berlin Wall separated East and West Russia. T F
3. The Wall of Troy is the subject of Homer's poem *The Odyssey*. T F
4. Hadrian's Wall was the northern border of the Roman Empire. T F

Writing

3 Look at the map on pages 76 and 77. Imagine you are taking an Interrail trip through Europe. In your notebook, describe your trip and include the following information.

- The countries you would like to visit and the order of your stops.
- The famous landmarks you would rather go to.
- The types of trains you would take.

Glossary

siege: the act of moving an army around a fortified place to capture it

nomadic: people who travel from place to place

pilgrimage: a long journey to a sacred place as an act of devotion

Unit 6

Vocabulary – Phrasal Verbs

1 Match each phrasal verb to its meaning.

0. tell on		a. to recover
1. own up		b. to confess
2. break up		c. to separate
3. get over		d. to report
4. go on		e. to discover
5. give up		f. to continue
6. figure out		g. to stop

2 Underline the sentence that describes each picture.

0

She's telling on her classmate. / She's owning up to her teacher.

1

They just got over it. / They just broke up.

2

He's trying to break up. / He wants to own up to what he did.

3

He's keeping the **gossip** to himself. / He's giving up.

4

My brother just goes on working. / My brother hasn't gotten over his ex-girlfriend.

5

I give up! / I figured it out.

Guess What!

Some phrasal verbs are separable.

A: Did you **figure out** the problem?
B: Yes, I **figured** it **out**!

Separable	Inseparable
turn (something) in	tell on
give (something) up	go on
get along (well) with	break up
figure (something) out	get over
keep (something) to (one)self	own up

Glossary

gossip: information about the personal lives of other people

3 Mark (✓) the type of phrasal verb in each sentence. Rewrite the sentence if the phrasal verb is separable.

	separable	inseparable
0. I have to turn in my homework before Friday.	✓	☐

I have to turn my homework in before Friday.

1. Jeff told on the bully after he hit him. ☐ ☐

_____

2. Lizzy figured out the riddle! ☐ ☐

_____

3. She had to give up running after she broke her leg. ☐ ☐

_____

Grammar – Modal Verbs for Possibility

1 In your notebook, write a sentence to describe each blurry picture. Use *might*, *could* or *may*.

0. This could be a train station or an airport.

2 Read the dilemmas. Write the possible solutions with *might*, *could* or *may*. See the grammar box on page 87.

Jenny is in the store with her best friend. She sees her friend pick up a pack of gum and put it in her pocket without paying. What does she do?

0. might: Jenny might talk to her friend about paying for the gum.
1. could: _____
2. may: _____

Michael saw one of his classmates pass a note to another classmate during their final exam. The teacher didn't see. Michael doesn't know what to do.

3. might: _____
4. could: _____
5. may: _____

Expressing Contrast

Words or Phrases to Express Contrast

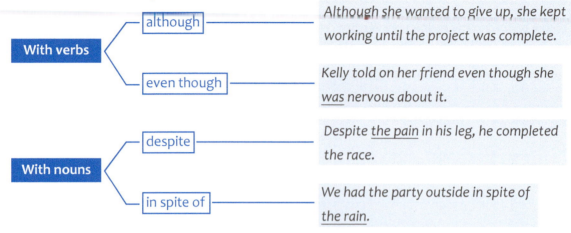

3 Rewrite the sentences using one of the words or phrases in the box above. More than one answer is possible.

   0. she was good at the guitar / she wanted to give up
      Although she was good at the guitar, she wanted to give up.
   1. many people didn't want to leave their homes / the hurricane warnings
      _____
   2. I grew up in a poor neighborhood / I went to college and became a professor
      _____
   3. Ben and Amanda broke up / they spent a lot of time together
      _____
   4. some bad grades / Jimena got into college
      _____

Review

1 Unscramble the sentences.

   0. tell / my / on / might / I / classmate / friend / he's / my / although
      I might tell on my classmate although he's my friend.
   1. may / Mike / they / Kelly / up / and / break / get along / well / even though
      _____
   2. not / over / get / Sally / parents' / her / divorce / could / counseling / the / despite
      _____
   3. just / could / it / keep / yourself / to / you /
      _____
   4. might / she / apologize / up / and / own
      _____

Reading

1 Read the article and write the numbers of the missing headings.

a. Make a pros and cons list
b. Analyze how your decision will affect others
c. Discuss your situation with a trusted person
d. Consider the credibility of your information source

Tips for Making Better Decisions

Have you ever been in a difficult position, made a decision and **regretted** it? Of course you have! Everyone has! What factors did you take into account to make the decision? We all make mistakes, but there are some ways to improve your decision-making skills in the future.

☐ **1** Did you get your information from someone who you trust or respect or does the person who gave you information **lie** or gossip a lot? Maybe the information you got is not reliable and you need to inform yourself more before you make a decision.

☐ **2** It's always a good idea to get an opinion from someone else or even from multiple people. Talk to someone you trust about the decision you have to make. You don't have to take their advice, but they may give you an idea you hadn't thought of before.

☐ **3** We all live in a community (family, school, neighborhood) and that means our decisions affect others. Think about how the consequences of your decisions may affect those around you. Take this into account before you make decisions.

☐ **4** When you have a difficult decision to make, it often helps to make a list of pros (the benefits of making a particular decision) and cons (the drawbacks). When you have a clear list of the positives and negatives of a decision, it is often clear which path to take. Be careful, the longest list doesn't mean the best decision. You also have to think about the **weight** of each positive or negative effect.

2 Read the dilemma. In your notebook, write the number of the tip(s) from the article you recommend and explain why.

Marcela wants to go to college, but she can't decide if she should go to college in her hometown or go away to college. If she stays home, she can be near her family, stay with friends and keep her part-time job. If she goes away, she can make new friends, learn independence, have new experiences and learn to cook for herself.

Writing

3 Follow the instructions.

1. Think about a dilemma you had in the past or you have in your life now.
2. In your notebook, describe your decision-making process. What did you do (or will you do) in order to solve the dilemma? Did you / Will you follow any of the tips above? Which ones? If you are writing about a decision in the past, do you regret it? How could you have made a better decision?
3. Use the phrasal verbs on page 85 and the words or phrases to express contrast on page 89.

Glossary

regret: to feel sorry or wish you hadn't done something you did

lie: to say something that is not true

weight: the influence or importance that something has

Unit 7

Vocabulary – Food Adjectives

1 Match the sentences.

0. I'm in the mood for something spicy.   ____ Chewy, not crispy.
1. My dad loves French fries.   ____ No. It's too sour!
2. How do you like your chocolate chip cookies?   _0_ Let's go get some hot wings.
3. What are some tasty ways to cook vegetables?   ____ Roasted, fried or grilled.
4. I love steamed dumplings.   ____ Doesn't he know baked potato is better for him?
5. Do you like lemon in your tea?   ____ Fried egg rolls are good, too!

2 Write the words below next to the food item that they describe.

~~spicy~~   chewy   salty   bland   sticky   sour

0. salsa   _spicy_
1. granola bar   _____
2. soup   _____
3. lemons   _____
4. bread   _____
5. honey   _____

3 Write the names of the dishes.

0. _Baklava_
1. _____
2. _____
3. _____
4. _____
5. _____
6. _____

4 Correct one mistake in each sentence.

0. To make French fries, you cut and steam potatoes.
   To make French fries you cut and fry potatoes.

1. At a barbeque it's common to bake meat.
   _____

2. My family likes to grill eggs in water instead of frying them in oil.
   _____

3. My aunt fries some great cakes and pies.
   _____

4. I can't cook! The only thing I can do is roast water.
   _____

5. My favorite food at a Chinese restaurant is the baked rice with eggs and vegetables.
   _____

5 **Complete the description of each dish from Activity 3.**

0. _British Sunday lunch_ is made up of meat and potatoes, vegetables, stuffing and Yorkshire pudding.
1. _____ can be steamed or fried and are filled with vegetables and meat.
2. _____ is raw fish and is popular in the coastal regions of Latin America.
3. _____ is a popular dish from India and is bright orange.
4. _____ is a fried bean patty that is popular in Brazil and West Africa.
5. _____ is a Turkish pastry made up of nuts, honey and filo dough.
6. _____ is a Hungarian meat stew seasoned with paprika that's eaten in Central and Eastern Europe.

Grammar – Present and Past Passive Voice

1 **Underline the verb and label each sentence A (Active) or P (Passive).**

0. The man <u>was informed</u> of the accident. **P**
1. A new restaurant was opened near the park.
2. My dad roasted some vegetables for dinner.
3. The school was founded in 1956.
4. Only grilled food was served at the party.
5. The kids ate all the spicy chicken wings at the party!

2 **Underline the correct option to complete the text.**

Thanksgiving, a US tradition

Every November my family (0) **celebrates** / **is celebrated** Thanksgiving. We (1) **make** / **were made** a giant meal and spend time together. We always talk about what we are thankful for in our lives. Here is a photo of our meal last year. The best part was the turkey, which (2) **roasted** / **was roasted** by my mom. The potatoes (3) **boiled** / **were boiled** by my brother and my sister (4) **baked** / **was baked** the bread. The green beans (5) **steam** / **were steamed** and I (6) **baked** / **was baked** a pie for dessert. It was a great meal!

Unit 7

3 Complete the sentences in the present or past passive using the verbs below.

invite   clean   steal   bake   cook   ~~tell~~

0. I _____was told_____ about the meeting too late to attend.
1. My bike _____ yesterday outside our house.
2. Sam _____ to the party, but he didn't come.
3. The house _____ on the weekends by the family.
4. To make this dish, the raw meat _____ on the grill along with the vegetables.
5. Cakes _____ every morning at the neighborhood bakery.

4 Read the sentences and choose when the doer is not important (NI) or when the doer is unknown (U).

0. Bananas are grown in the Philippines. Sugar is too!   (NI)   U
1. The house was burned to the ground in the fire. The family is now homeless.   NI   U
2. The bank was robbed yesterday. Police are still searching for the suspect.   NI   U
3. Over 800 languages are spoken in Papua New Guinea. That's more than any other country in the world.   NI   U
4. Newspapers are read online nowadays.   NI   U
5. The money was donated anonymously. We'll never know who gave it.   NI   U

Review

1 Look and mark the statements T (True) or F (False). Correct the false statements.

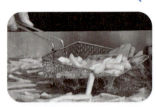

0. The potato was baked.   T   (F)
   The potato was fried.

1. The green beans were steamed.   T   F
   _____

2. The eggs were fried.   T   F
   _____

3. The meat was roasted.   T   F
   _____

4. The fish was grilled.   T   F
   _____

5. The chicken was roasted.   T   F
   _____

Cooking for Better Health

Reading

1 Circle the types of cooking food that are popular in your community.

boiling   steaming   frying   baking   grilling   roasting

2 Read the text. Then mark each statement T (True) or F (False). In your notebook, correct the false statements.

Did you know that different styles of cooking are more popular in different cultures? For instance, in the south of the United States, fried foods are very common such as fried chicken, fried fish and even fried green tomatoes! At state or county **fairs** they even sell fried Oreos!

But frying food is very unhealthy. It adds a lot of fat and calories to your meal and it reduces the nutrients in your food. Baking food is a much better option. Take a baked potato, for instance. It has **roughly** 220 calories and 1 gram of fat, but if you take that same potato and cut it up in to French fries and fry it, it has 700 calories and 34 grams of fat! What about boiling versus steaming? Do you know which one is healthier? If you guessed steaming, you are correct. It's not that boiling food adds fat or calories to your food like frying; it's the opposite problem. It takes away vitamins, minerals and other nutritious **properties**.

Take broccoli, for example; it is usually boiled. That way it gets clean too, but washing it thoroughly and steaming it is the healthier way. It preserves the color, taste and nutrients and keeps it crunchy! Grilling food is also a healthy option but be sure not to eat anything that has been burned. It contains chemicals that can increase your risk of cancer. While cooking some foods **brings out** their nutrients, some foods are best for you when they are not cooked at all but are eaten raw. Peppers and onions are examples of two foods that offer more nutrients when eaten raw. Just be sure to brush your teeth afterwards!

0. Steaming food is very popular in the southern US.	T	**F**
Frying food is very popular in the southern US.		
1. Eating burned food can increase your risk of diabetes.	T	F
2. Broccoli and potatoes are better for you if you eat them raw.	T	F
3. Steaming food preserves more nutrients than boiling.	T	F
4. A baked potato is healthier than a fried one.	T	F

Writing

3 In your notebook, answer the following questions. Then use that information to write a reflection on how food is prepared in your family.

1. Is the food prepared in your family healthy? Why or why not?
2. Why does your family prepare food the way they do?
3. What changes can your family make to prepare food in a more nutritious way?
4. Give examples to illustrate your points.

Glossary

fair: a public event, usually held outside, where goods are shown and sold, and where there is often food and entertainment

roughly: approximately

properties: qualities or characteristics of something

bring out: to cause to occur or exist

Unit 8

Vocabulary – Unusual Jobs

1 Look and write the jobs.

0. crime scene investigator

1. _____

2. _____

3. _____

4. _____

2 Read and write the jobs.

0. whistle / uniform / motivation — sports coach
1. police tape / fingerprints / photos — _____
2. movies / actors / scenes — _____
3. walls / urban / spray paint — _____
4. endangered species / scientific method — _____
5. flights / deadlines / bed and breakfast — _____
6. audio / graphics / code — _____
7. knives / oven / seasoning — _____

3 Match the words to their definitions.

0. retire — e
1. qualification — ___
2. apply — ___
3. deal with — ___
4. manage — ___
5. contract — ___
6. earn — ___

a. to take action to do something, especially to solve a problem
b. to make an official request for a job, place in a university
c. an ability, experience, or quality that you need in order to do a particular job or activity
d. to organize and control the work of a company or group of people
e. to stop working, especially because of age
f. to receive money for work that you do
g. a written legal agreement between two people or businesses

4 Choose words from Activity 3 and fill in the mind maps below. Add more words if necessary.

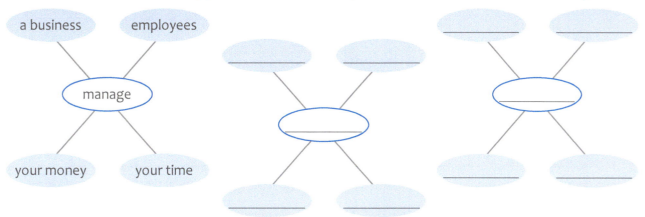

Grammar – Relative Clauses

1 Read the relative clauses and write D (Defining) or ND (Non-defining).

0. This book, which my mom gave me, is excellent! — ND
1. My aunt, who is an animation director, is coming to visit for my birthday. ____
2. An art director is a person who designs scenes for movies and videos. ____
3. Radiology technicians are professionals who take X-rays and other scans. ____
4. This is the restaurant that has great hamburgers. ____
5. Ms. Smith, who coaches tennis, is a great teacher. ____

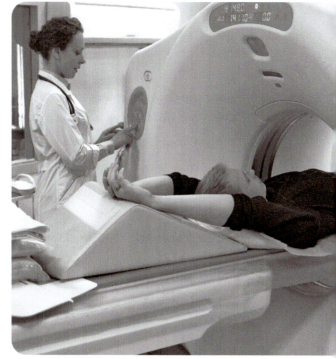

2 Rewrite the sentences using relative clauses. Include commas where necessary.

0. Lacrosse is a sport. It uses a ball and sticks with nets.
   Lacrosse is a sport which uses a ball and sticks with nets.
1. A botanist is a type of scientist. They study plants.
   _____
2. My dad is very competitive. He won employee of the month.
   _____
3. Mr. Kelly is the school principal. He's from France.
   _____
4. Engineers are in demand. They design materials, structures and systems.
   _____
5. The career of speech pathology deals with communication disorders. It's a growing field.
   _____

Unit 8

3 Correct one mistake in each sentence and rewrite it.

0. A career interest survey is a tool ~~who~~ helps you figure out what careers may be a good choice for you in the future.
   A career interest survey is a tool that helps you figure out what careers may be a good choice for you in the future.

1. A school counselor is a person, who gives advice about career opportunities.
   _____

2. An interpreter, is a great career for bilinguals, involves spoken language.
   _____

3. Human resources professionals are specialists which help companies find qualified employees.
   _____

4. My dream which is to be an actor is a difficult one to achieve.
   _____

5. Accountants are people, who prepare and examine financial records.
   _____

4 Read the defining relative clauses and write S (Subject relative clause) or O (Object relative clause). Cross out the relative pronouns that can be omitted.

0. I have an idea ~~that~~ you would love.   __O__
1. It's important to research any job that you are interested in.   ____
2. Mexico is a country that has a growing economy.   ____
3. The psychiatrist who you saw last week is Ms. Pérez.   ____
4. They gave my friend the job that I wanted.   ____
5. They canceled the class which I really wanted to take.   ____
6. The teacher who supervises the chess team retired.   ____

Review

1 Complete the job descriptions using relative clauses.

0. A marine biologist is a person *who studies aquatic life*.
1. A chef is a person _____.
2. A sports coach is a person _____.
3. A graffiti artist is a person _____.
4. A travel writer is a person _____.
5. An animation director is a person _____.
6. A computer game programmer is a person _____.
7. A crime scene investigator is a person _____.

Consider a Career in Health Care

If you are like most teens, you haven't yet decided on the career you want to have after you graduate. Of course you want to do something you like, but it's important to consider other factors like job security, flexibility and options for growth.

In many countries, jobs in health care are in demand. This is because the world's population is growing and as people get older they need more care. This has created an urgent need for health care professionals and this need will only continue to grow. Doctors and nurses are common health care jobs, but there are many others that are well paid and in demand. Here are just a few you might consider.

Radiology Technician: This is a specialist who takes X-rays and other types of scans that allow doctors to make informed decisions about their patients.

Physical Therapist: These are health care professionals who work with patients who have a physical condition that they are treating. It may be an injury a patient is recovering from or challenges dealing with the effects of aging on the body.

Lab Technician: This is a technician who analyzes lab work including tissue and blood samples. The information helps doctors give patients informed recommendations.

A job in health care may be a great option for you. You can work in the private or public sector, in schools or hospitals or in your own practice. You also will have flexibility in where you live since health care professionals are needed in most places.

Jobs in health care are open to people of all education levels, but most require at least some training after high school. Many require a college degree as well as **postgraduate** work. It all depends on the specific career you want to pursue and the qualifications accepted in your country. If you are interested, ask your teachers or counselors for more information.

Reading

1 Read the article and mark (✓) the health care career you prefer.
   ☐ Radiology Technician
   ☐ Physical Therapist
   ☐ Lab Technician

2 Answer the following questions.

1. Why are jobs in health care so in demand?

   _____

2. What is one benefit of a health care job?

   _____

3. What qualifications for a health care job are mentioned in the article?

   _____

Writing

3 In your notebook, write a paragraph about your dream job. Include the following information.
   - A topic sentence that states what your dream job is.
   - Supporting sentences that explain the qualifications you need for your dream job, the responsibilities, the rewards and where you would work.
   - A conclusion that states why you want this job.

Glossary

postgraduate: studies after getting a bachelor's degree, graduate studies towards a Master's degree or Doctorate.

Just for Fun Answer Key

Unit 1
1 1. jazz 2. classical 3. rap 4. reggae 5. country 6. rock 7. latin 8. pop
2 1. moving 2. loud 3. relaxing 4. dramatic 5. catchy 6. inspiring
Mystery word: guitar
3 1. He is as fast as an ostrich. 2. He is as strong as an elephant. 3. He is as clever as Einstein. 4. He is as tall as a gorilla. 5. He is as brave as a lion. 6. He is as quiet as a mouse.

Unit 2
1 1. overnight in the mall 2. pig 3. nose 4. in a math class 5. fish 6. bird 7. face 8. month
2 *From top to bottom:* been, drunk, had, brought, thought, put, driven, read, broken, written
3 1. eaten 2. broken 3. met 4. found 5. traveled 6. seen
4 Answers will vary.

Unit 3
1 *From left to right:* hang up the clothes, put away the clothes, take out the trash, do the dishes, No chores!, walk the dog
2 *Counter clockwise:* 5, 3, 2, 1, 4
3 French, Thai, Swiss, Spanish, Peruvian, Pakistani, Dutch, Chilean, Greek, Icelandic, Colombian, Mexican

Unit 4
1 1. c 2. d 3. b 4. a
2 3
3 Answers will vary.

Unit 5
1 *From left to right:* shorts, sunglasses, stuffed animal, toothpaste, toothbrush, shirt cap, socks, evil eye, pen, keys, pajamas, sneakers, Cuba travel guide, pyramid, bottle of water, sandals, sunscreen
2 1. too 2. enough 3. enough 4. enough 5. too 6. too
3 Answers will vary.

Unit 6
1 1. get over 2. turn in 3. give up 4. tell on 5. break up 6. go on 7. figure out 8. keep to yourself 9. own up 10. get along with
2 Answers will vary.
3 1. Julia Roberts 2. Tom Hiddlestone 3. James Corden 4. Adele

Unit 7
1 *From top to bottom:* 4, 3, 2, 1
2 *From left to right:* beef, goulash, croissant, pie, butter, pancake, baklava, acaraje, dumplings, turkey
3 1
4 *From left to right:* eggs, oatmeal, mushrooms, cheese, meat, milk, peanuts, apples, carrots, tomatoes, green beans, avocado, chicken breast

Unit 8
1 *Across:* crime scene investigator *Down:* sports coach, chef, marine biologist, graffiti artist, travel writer, animation director
2 1. Cristeta Comerford 2. Andrew Stanton 3. Susan Wojcick 4. Ishai Golan

Grammar Reference

Unit 7

As ... As

We use *as ... as* to say two things are equal or the same. We use *as* + adjective + *as* with nouns.

- London is **as big as** Paris.
- I'm **as old as** Jim.

We use (*not*) *as ... as* to say two things are not the same.

- I'm **not as old as** Sarah. Sarah's 13. I'm 12.

When a pronoun follows *as ... as*, we use the object form.

- Jim is as old as **me**.
- I'm as fast as **them**.

We can also use *as ... as* to compare gerunds (-ing).

- Running is as good as **jogging**.
- Dancing isn't as popular as **swimming**.

Unit 2

Present Perfect with *How long? For, Since*

We use the present perfect to talk about our life experiences up to now. It refers to an action that started in the past and continues into the present.

- **How long** have you **been** in this school?
- I **have been** in this school for five years.

Note: the time period is not finished. We are thinking about the time period, not the action.

Finished Time Periods (Past Simple)	Unfinished Time Periods (Present Perfect)
in 2016 yesterday last year 2 weeks ago	ever never since Thursday

We form the present perfect with *have / has* + the past participle of the verb.

- I **have been** to New York three times.
- She **has finished** her homework.

Most regular past participles are the same as the past simple.

- Grandpa **has traveled** all around the world.
- It **has rained** every day this week.

Irregular verbs take several different forms in the past participle.

- She's **written** a book!
- You've **never won** a soccer match.

To form negative sentences, we add *not* to the auxiliary verb *have*.

- I **have not been** to New York.
- She **hasn't finished** her homework.

To form Yes / No questions, the auxiliary *have* goes at the beginning.

- **Have** you **been** to New York?
- **Has** she **finished** her homework?

For short answers to Yes / No questions, we use the auxiliary *have*.

- Have you been to New York?
  Yes, **I have**. / No, **I haven't**.
- Has she finished her homework?
  Yes, she **has**. / No, she **hasn't**.

We can use the present perfect with *how long* in questions.

- **How long** has Jackie been in your class?
- **How long** have you lived in your apartment?

We use *for* and *since* with the present perfect to say how long we do actions. We use *for* with a period of time.

- Jackie has been in my class **for** four months.
- We've lived in our apartment **for** five years.

We use *since* with the beginning of a period of time.

- Jackie has been in my class **since** January.
- We've lived in our apartment **since** 2014.

Past Perfect

We use the past perfect with the past simple. We use the past perfect for an earlier past action.
- The teacher was angry because we **hadn't done** the homework.
- When I got home, my sister **had gone** to bed.

We form the past perfect with *had* + the past participle.
- Grandma said "thank you" because I **had helped** her in the supermarket.
- Lisa called me because she **had seen** me on TV.

Note that the past perfect of *have* is *had had*.
- I was happy because **I had had** some good news.

To form negative sentences, we add *not* to the auxiliary verb *had*.
- We lost the game because we **had not played** well.
- Jim felt hungry because he **had not** eaten breakfast.

To form Yes / No questions, the auxiliary *had* goes at the beginning.
- **Had** the shops **closed** before you arrived?
- **Had** you **spoken** to Frank before he came to the party?

For short answers to Yes / No questions, we use the auxiliary *had*.
- Had the shops closed before you arrived?
  Yes, they **had**. / No, they **hadn't**.
- Had you spoken to Frank before he came to the party?
  Yes, I **had**. / No, I **hadn't**.

Unit 4

Second Conditional

We use the second conditional to talk about imaginary, unreal or impossible situations.
- If I **were** an animal, I **would** be a tiger.
- I **would** go to the moon if I **had** a spaceship.

We form the second conditional with **if** + past simple + *would* + infinitive.
- If I **lived** in the mountains, I **would** go skiing every day.

We use *would* + infinitive without *to* in the second part of the sentence.
- If I **walked** under a ladder, I **would have** seven years' bad luck!

We can put the *if-* clause first or second in the sentence. This does not change the meaning. If the *if-* clause appears first, we put a comma (,) between the two parts of the sentence.
- If I saw a four-leaved clover, I would have good luck.
- I would have good luck if I saw a four-leaved clover.

We can use **was** or **were** in the *if*-clause with *I, he, she, it*.
- If I were English, I'd live in London.
- If I was English, I'd live in London.
- Karen would be at school today if she weren't in the hospital.
- Karen would be at school today if she wasn't in the hospital.

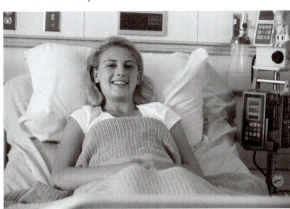

Preferences

We use *would like* + infinitive to talk about our preferences.

- *I **would like** to go to France.*
- *Mary **would like** to go to Easter Island.*

To form negative sentences, we add *not* to the auxiliary verb *would*.

- *She **would not like** to see a science fiction movie.*
- *I **would not like** to have bacon and eggs for breakfast.*

We also use *would rather* + infinitive without *to* to talk about our preferences.

- *Would you **rather play** basketball or baseball?*
  *We would **rather play** basketball.*
- *Would you **rather go** to the beach or stay in the hotel?*
  *I would **rather go** to the beach.*

To form negative sentences, we use *would rather not* + infinitive without *to*.

- *Why did you call Molly after school?*
  *I would **rather not** say.*

In a response, *would rather not* is often used without the verb.

- *Would your brother like to sing at the school show?*
  He'd rather not, actually.

We use *would prefer* + infinitive to talk about our preferences. We can use *prefer* when we have two or more options.

- *Would you like to meet on Tuesday, Wednesday or Thursday?*
  *I **would prefer to** meet on Thursday.*
- *Would you like to play a game or watch TV?*
  *I **would prefer to** play a game.*

To form negative sentences, we use *prefer not* + infinitive.

- *Would you prefer to stay in a campsite or at a youth hostel?*
  *I'd **prefer not to** stay at a youth hostel.*
- *Would you prefer to have music or English classes after school?*
  *I'd **prefer not to** have music lessons.*

Too and Enough

We use *too* when there is an excess of something.

- *I have **too** much homework this afternoon.*

We use *too* + adjective / adverb or *too* + *much* / *many* + noun.

To form negative sentences, we use auxiliary verb *do* + *not* + infinitive without *to* + *too*

- *I **don't have** too much homework this afternoon.*

To form Yes / No questions, we use the auxiliary verb *do*.

- ***Do** you have too much homework this afternoon?*

We use *enough* when there is as much as is necessary.

- *I have **enough** money to buy a new cell phone.*

We use adjective / adverb + *enough* or *enough* + noun.

To form negative sentences, we use auxiliary verb *do* + *not* + infinitive without *to* + *enough*

- *I **don't have** enough money to buy a new cell phone.*

To form Yes / No questions, we use the auxiliary verb *do*.

- ***Do** you have enough money to buy a cell phone?*

Unit 6

Might, Could, May for possibility

Could, *may* and *might* are modal auxiliary verbs. We use *could*, *may* and *might* + infinitive without *to* to talk about possibility. *Might* is the least possible. *Could* is more possible and *may* is even more possible.

- We **might** go to the party because it's raining a lot.
- We **could** go to the party because it's raining less.
- We **may** go to the party because it almost stopped raining.

To make negative sentences, we add *not* to the auxiliaries *may* and *might*. *May* and *might* mean "perhaps not."

- It might **not** snow next week.
- We may **not** win the game

We use *can't* + infinitive without *to* to say something is not possible (there is a 0% possibility).

- It **can't** rain tomorrow.

We ask questions about possibility using *could* and *might*. *Could* is more common than *might* in questions.

- **Could** we win the game tomorrow?
- **Might** it rain next week?

We do not use *may* in questions to ask about possibility.

- ~~May it rain next week?~~

Unit 7

The Passive

Normal verbs are in the active voice. The subject does the action.
- *Dad makes lunch.*
- *I wrote that e-mail.*

In passive sentences, the subject receives the action.
- *Lunch is made by Dad.*
- *Those e-mails are written by me.*

We often use the passive when we don't know or don't care who does the action.
- *These jeans **are made** in the US.*
- *French **is spoken** in many different countries.*

We make the present passive with *be* + the past participle.

I	am	taught
You	are	taught
He / She / It	is	taught
We	are	taught
They	are	taught

- *I **am driven** to school.*
- *Our class **is taught** in English.*

We use *by* + person to say who does the passive action.
- *I am driven to school **by my mom**.*
- *Our class is taught in English **by Ms. Scott**.*

To make negative sentences, we add *not* to the auxiliary verb *be*.
- *Our team isn't coached by Mr. Johnson.*
- *These books aren't sold in the shop.*

To make Yes / No questions, the auxiliary *be* goes at the beginning.
- ***Is** your class taught by Ms. Scott?*
- ***Are** your friends invited to the party?*

For short answers to Yes / No questions, we use the auxiliary *is / are*.
- ***Is** your class **taught** by Ms. Scott?
Yes, it **is**. / No, it **isn't**.*
- ***Are** your friends **invited** to the party?
Yes, they **are**. / No, they **aren't**.*

We make the past passive with *was / were* + the past participle.

I	was	taught
You	were	taught
He / She / It	was	taught
We	were	taught
They	were	taught

- *I **was taught** by Mr. Peters last year.*

To make negative sentences, we add *not* to the auxiliary verb *was / were*.
- *Dom wasn't **helped** by his parents.*

To make Yes / No questions, the auxiliary *was / were* goes at the beginning.
- ***Was** your package delivered yesterday?*
- ***Were** these photos taken by you?*

For short answers to Yes / No questions, we use the auxiliary *was / were*.
- *Was your package delivered yesterday?
Yes, it **was**. / No, it **wasn't**.*
- *Were these photos taken by you?
Yes, they **were**. / No, they **weren't**.*

Defining and Non-defining Relative Clauses

We use defining relative clauses to say exactly what a noun is.

- *Shazam is an app **that recognizes songs**.*
- *Alexander Graham Bell is the person **who invented the telephone**.*

We use *who* or *that* to define or describe a person.

- *A burglar is a person **who** steals from houses and people's homes.*
- *This is the girl **that** has just joined our class.*

We use *which* or *that* to define or describe a person or a thing.

- *A cronut is a type of bread **that** is half-croissant and half-donut.*

Who, *which* and *that* are relative pronouns. If the relative pronoun is the object of a defining relative clause, we can omit it.

- *James is the person **(who)** I met at the training camp.*
- *Travel writing is the job **(which)** Nick wants to do.*

We use non-defining relative clauses to give extra information about a noun. We use commas before and after a non-defining relative clause.

- *This photo, **which I love**, was taken by my mom.*
- *My sister, **who you met yesterday**, is a graffiti artist.*

We cannot use *that* to replace *who* or *which* in a non-defining relative clause.

Verb List

Present	Past	Past Participle	Present	Past	Past Participle
bake	baked	baked	pour	poured	poured
bark	barked	barked	put	put	put
be	was / were	been	retire	retired	retired
board	boarded	boarded	ride	rode	ridden
boil	boiled	boiled	roast	roasted	roasted
break	broke	broken	run	ran	run
earn	earned	earned	send	sent	sent
feed	fed	fed	sing	sang	sung
feel	felt	felt	sit	sat	sat
find	found	found	snore	snored	snored
forget	forgot	forgotten	spend	spent	spent
fry	fried	fried	spill	spilled	spilled
grill	grilled	grilled	sponsor	sponsored	sponsored
grow	grew	grown	steal	stole	stolen
hang	hung	hung	steam	steamed	steamed
hold	held	held	sweep	swept	swept
keep	kept	kept	think	thought	thought
know	knew	known	throw	threw	thrown
learn	learned / learnt	learned / learnt	understand	understood	understood
leave	left	left	wear	wore	worn
lose	lost	lost	wipe	wiped	wiped
meet	met	met	write	wrote	written

Phrasal Verbs

break up: to end a relationship

clean *sth out: to make a place clean by removing all the objects that you don't need

clean *sth up: to make a place completely clean, especially if it is dirty

figure *sth out: to solve a problem or find an answer

get along with: to be friends with someone

get over: to recover from a bad experience

give *sth up: to stop doing something

go on: to continue doing

hang *sth up: to put clothes on a coat hanger and put them in a closet

keep *sth to (myself): not to share some information with other people

own up: to confess you did a crime or broke a rule

pick *sth up (1): to clean and tidy a room, especially a bedroom

pick *sth up (2): to collect your luggage after you get off a plane

put *sth away: to place an object inside a closet, desk, etc. after you use it

take *sth out: to move something out of a house, building or room

tell on **so: to report someone to a parent or teacher for breaking a rule

throw *sth away: to put something in the trash because you don't need it

turn **so in: to report a criminal to the police

wipe *sth off: to clean a dirty surface with a wet cloth

* something   ** someone